Hippocrene U.S.A. Guide to

EXPLORING THE
LITCHFIELD HILLS

CANOEING ON THE HOUSATONIC

Hippocrene U.S.A. Guide to

EXPLORING THE LITCHFIELD HILLS

In Six Tours

by

Herbert S. Whitman
Illustrated by Rosemary Fox

HIPPOCRENE BOOKS
New York

For information, address:
HIPPOCRENE BOOKS, INC.
171 Madison Avenue
New York, NY 10016

ISBN 0-7818-0045-5

Library of Congress Cataloging-in-Publication Data available.

Printed in the United States of America.

Dedication

To my daughter Ronalda Whitman, whose devotion to me made this book possible. I dedicate *Exploring the Litchfield Hills* to her with all my love.

The long months of research that went into this book were made pleasant by the willing help of many people. To them all I owe a deep debt of gratitude.

They are Mary Campbell, Sabrina Lietzmann, Sally Ellsworth, Pamela Wyeth, Charles Olivea, Leo Hulton, James Hulton, Mark McEachern, Ernest Ceder, Barbara Thorland, Alan Dodd, Elmer Worthington, William Bader, Emily Hopson, Virginia Moskowitz, Howard Slayman, John Lorenzo, Marion Stock, Sylvia Wismar, Lisa Trent, John Trent, Cay Fields, Francis Frattini, Margaret Wood, Frederick Strong, Barbara Heim, Mary Harwood, Leona Shelton, Elizabeth McNeill, Susan Branson, Pat Zeitler, Frances Crowell, Charles Buell, Bruce Mosher, Marion Thierry, Susan Stephenson, Anita Canfield, Vaughn Gray, Jill Carr, Malcomb Hunt, Anne Wahlberg, Naneen Bunnell, Alice Meade, John Sanderson, George Sherwood, Walter France, Ernest Anderson, and William Nelson.

INSIDE SCHOOLHOUSE, GAYLORDSVILLE

CONTENTS

FOURTH TOUR
Page 91
*The fourth tour of exploration begins in
the Litchfield Hills in the pretty little town of
Bridgewater in the southwest corner of the county.
Then it goes to Roxbury and on to
Washington and Washington Depot.*

FIFTH TOUR
Page 109
*The fifth tour starts in Bristol, in the far southeast
corner. After going through Terryville, Plymouth,
Thomaston, Watertown, and Woodbury,
it goes north to Bethlehem and ends in Morris.*

SIXTH TOUR
Page 135
*The sixth and last tour begins in Goshen. It goes to
Torrington and Harwinton, then to Riverton,
Winsted, and Colebrook, and ends in storied Norfolk.*

INTRODUCTION

WAY UP IN THE NORTHEAST CORNER OF LITCHFIELD County are the Colebrook River Reservoir, Riverton, two big state forests, and the mini-city of Winsted. In the southeast is Watertown, then Woodbury, Roxbury, Bridgewater and finally, New Milford. In this historic region we shall launch our adventure of exploring the Litchfield Hills with Indian legends, history, and curiosities along the way. We won't dwell on the wonder and beauty of the Litchfield Hills, but put you on your way. You don't have to follow these tours. Go where you like and use this book only when you feel like it.

One other thing. Don't fret about getting lost. All explorers get lost. Columbus did. On his way over here he didn't have the foggiest notion where he was or where he was going. You are an explorer too. That's the fun of it. Some of the most interesting things you will come upon will be the back roads you didn't expect. All roads go some place.

FIRST TOUR

The first tour begins in Bridgewater, goes to New Milford,
up to Route 7 to Gaylordsville, to Kent Falls and Kent.

"A HIDEOUS, HOWLING WILDERNESS," WAS HOW THE REV.
Benjamin Wadsworth described the virgin forests of Litchfield
County when he rode into what is now New Milford in 1694,
where the trees were so close together that in some places a
horse couldn't squeeze through.

There were not many Indians in Mr. Wadsworth's time
because the warlike Mohawks from across the Hudson came
over on raiding parties exacting tribute. The locals fled north
towards Kent and settled there. They were Schaghticokes. Poor
people, they had a miserable time, not only from the Mohawks,
but from the white settlers, who kept stealing their land. But
the Indians stuck it out and their descendants are still there.

Mr. Wadsworth in his journal left no doubt that settling in
this primeval region was tough going, but despite this, settlers
bought big tracts of land when they were up for auction, loaded
their horses and their families and set off into an unknown land
with nothing in it but a scattering of Indians and wild beasts.
Courageous and determined people they were, undaunted by
hardship. They were made of good stuff.

Litchfield County, rich in history and legend and year-round beauty, is in the northwest corner of Connecticut. Its northern border is Berkshire County, Massachusetts, and on the west is New York. Its east boundary is Hartford County and is anything but straight. On the south are Fairfield and New Haven counties, also wiggly.

Before we go any further, we recommend you buy a map called *Litchfield County*, put together with great care by master map-maker Vaughn Gray. Around its borders are neat drawings in precise detail of historic buildings and places. The map is on parchment-like paper so tough you can fold and unfold it many times before it shows signs of wear. You can buy it in many stores in Litchfield County.

South of New Milford the Housatonic River widens out to form Lake Lillinonah, named for the daughter of powerful Chief Waramaug, the big wheel in those parts. Chief Waramaug and his family lived in what must have been the biggest and showiest house for miles around. It was said to be 100 feet long on a promontory high over the river at a place that came to be called Lover's Leap, the scene of the tragedy we are about to relate to you. We'd better tell you first how to get there.

At the south end of the New Milford green is Bridge Street. Go east (left), then right on Route 67 and almost immediately right on Grove Street. Two miles later is a bridge over the river. Avoid it and keep going a short way to another bridge, an old iron thing blocked off. Park and follow a path through the woods, a fairly long walk up the promontory where the chief's house stood long ago. The view down the river is sensational, a great picture.

A steep bank precipitates sharply down through the hemlocks to a gorge in the river, which the current courses swiftly through because it's so narrow. A short way down, centuries ago, the river boiled over a dam, now sunk deep beneath the surface.

Like most legends about beautiful Indian princesses, the story of Lillinonah is sad indeed. Walking in the woods one day

WAMPANOAG INDIAN

PRINCESS LILLINONAH

collecting dog-toothed violets, Lillinonah came upon a young
white man, a startling sight because white people didn't venture
so far north from the coast. The two palled around together and
soon a magnetism lit their lights. The young man was captivated
by Lilli's beauty; Lilli took her conquest home to show him off
to Pa. Pa, realizing what was going on, was perplexed at the
thought of a white son-in-law and sought the advice of the Great

Spirit. The Great Spirit approved, so Pa told the young man that he could stick around until winter. When winter approached, the young man kissed his girl goodbye and left, promising to come back in the spring. Spring came. No young man. Poor Lilli's pining touched her father's heart and, thinking that he would get everything fixed up, he asked Eagle Feather, a young brave of the tribe, to marry Lilli. Being a dutiful daughter, Lilli consented.

On the day of the wedding, Lilli put on the bridal gown of a princess with feathered earrings, and vowing to herself that she would never marry anyone but her lover, she vanished into the hemlocks and raced through the woods to where she had hidden her canoe.

High drama unfolded. The youth, late getting finished with his work on his family's farm on the coast, ran through the woods as fast as he could with the premonition that he'd better hurry. He panted all the way up the path to the promontory, and looking down, he saw to his horror that the canoe with Lilli in it was headed right for the falls. Lilli looked up. Their eyes met. Without hesitating, the young man took a mighty leap and splashed down right beside Lilli's canoe. Lilli bailed out. They embraced, and in a moment they disappeared in the mists over the Great Falls. We presume, nay, we hope, that they were married in the arms of the Great Spirit.

In those days the water in the gorge was 70 feet lower than it is now, so the young man's leap was 140 feet!

Lake Lillinonah and its visitors are well taken care of by the state of Connecticut which patrols the lake during heavy traffic hours. You will find boat launches at Route 133 and the bridge at Bridgewater, also at Pond Road in Newtown. There are more boat launches in Roxbury at the end of Falls Road, in Southbury off West Purchase Road, at the end of Hanover Road in Newtown, and off Grove Street in New Milford.

There are two marinas on Lake Lillinonah, one at the end of

LAKE LILLINONAH, NEW MILFORD

Cooper Road called Driftwood, and the other at the end of West Street in New Milford. It is on the grounds of the old J. P. Stevens factory and is Fischel Marina.

New Milford, the largest town in Litchfield County, takes some doing because it's so varied and interesting. It was called Weantinock by the Indians, who sold it in 1703 to a group of white men from Milford. We think you will find a walking tour of New Milford pleasant, with shops to browse in and pictures to take.

Route 67 will take you into the ancient part of the town. It has one of the longest greens in the county, wide and a quarter of a mile long, bounded on both sides by Main Street. Substantial colonial houses run its length. One of them is the Town Hall, and on its site was the home of Roger Sherman, the only man to sign all four great charters of American Liberty: the Articles of Association (1774), the Declaration of Independence (1776), the Articles of Confederation (1777) and the United States Constitution (1787).

At the end of the green is the New Milford Historical Society and Museum. We are sure that you have noticed in your travels around Litchfield County that most towns, even small ones, have created historical societies and museums, vital and loving places where the townspeople have preserved their treasures for others to enjoy, their pictures and silverware, their ancient uniforms and baby buggies, their history in glass cases, the rooms where they have their meetings, lectures and suppers.

Such is the little brick building on Aspetuck Avenue. It is presided over by Malcomb Hunt, a friendly and knowledgeable man, who will see that you are guided through the exhibits. The society has a fine collection of portraits of New Milford people, many by the famous and prolific artist Ralph Earl. The society's number is (203) 354-3069.

There's not much noise from trains these days because there are so few of them, only an occasional freight. Railroad Street is a good place for browsing, especially a store called Connecticut Memories. If you ask somebody what it sells you'll just get a laugh. The store is crammed with every imaginable thing. To list them all would be futile. It's bewildering. The things spill out into the street. It's a pack-rat's paradise.

If you want to see a lovely place, go north on Aspetuck Avenue

NEW MILFORD LIBRARY

beyond the top end of the green, and you will come to the Canterbury School, which derives its name from an English school established by St. Dunstan, archbishop of Canterbury in the 10th century. It is a college preparatory school on a big, beautiful campus with handsome buildings and outstanding views.

The benevolence of Eliot Pratt years ago created one of the most appealing places around. It's an education center that bears his name. We recommend you get involved, you and your children. It's a few miles north of New Milford on the west side of Route 202 down a curving driveway. The headquarters is a modest house, but what goes on there is anything but modest.

The center is family-oriented. There is a farm where you can pet the animals, a wildlife workshop, and field trips where you can get your feet wet in wetlands and study the things that go in swamps, things like bullfrogs, salamanders, dragonflies, snakes, turtles, and tadpoles, in season, of course.

There is a workshop where you can study wildlife habitats, flood control, groundwater use, that sort of thing. An astronomer will teach you what goes on in the heavens, and relate ancient star legends. If you bring a lens from an old copying machine, you can learn to make your own telescope. You can learn about grasslands management and how to run a dairy farm.

There are one-week and two-week programs for children, where they wake up to a day filled with activities, outdoor cooking, a river ramble, a walk to learn about useful plants. "We strive," they say, "to provide a safe outdoor program that teaches children how to appreciate nature."

Starting at the headquarters building are lovely, well-marked trails which you may hike any time. The telephone in (203) 355-3137. If you think you are qualified for a summer job, call Cathy Setterlin, the executive director.

To continue up Route 202 will run into the fourth tour so we shall go back to New Milford.

The old railroad station, a block west of the green, is now, among other things, the busy and useful Chamber of Commerce, presided over by Pat Hembrook, a pleasant and efficient lady who will answer your questions about the area. Her number is (203) 354-6080.

There is a fine bed and breakfast on Elm Street several blocks east of the green called the Homestead. The number is (203) 354-4080.

Teddy Roosevelt made a brief speech from the back of his train as it whistle-stopped beside the Heritage Inn on Bridge Street in 1906. The little hotel is clean and well-run. The number is (203) 354-8883.

New Milford must be some kind of paradise for gastronomes. There are 42 restaurants from high-grade to ho-hum and we shall mention only a few at the top. Up Route 7 a mile or so is Maison Le Blanc. The *New York Times* says of it, "Deserves cheers," and *Connecticut Magazine* says, "Best French restaurant in Litchfield County." The house is old and charming and the grounds go down to the river. It's expensive. The number is (203) 354-9931. Several others on our list are on Route 202 going north from New Milford. Le Bon Coin is an excellent French restaurant with a mouth-watering menu. *The Hartford Courant* says, "The food sings at Carole Peck's restaurant," and the *Litchfield County Times* says, "Carole Peck is a chef for all seasons." Her number is (203) 355-1310.

Rudy's is owned and run by Pauline and Peter Lang, The restaurant is year-round and welcomes people who live in the area as well as passers-by. The food is good and the prices moderate. The number is (203) 354-7727.

North of New Milford on Route 7 is the Connecticut Maple Leaf Motor Lodge whose land also goes right down to the river so you can go fishing and boating there. There's plenty of space for reunions with grills and picnic tables under the trees. Marie Milla is the owner of this well-run bed and breakfast. The number is (203) 354-2633.

A short way south of New Milford is McDonalds. The road next to it is Sunny Valley Road. We urge you to take it because it leads to the Sunny Valley Foundation, a non-profit, tax-exempt organization devoted to the preservation of agriculture in the northeastern states. Go left, then right to signs directing you to it. The foundation is a noble enterprise, but we take you there not for its work but for its 2000 acres of farms, woodlands, and hiking trails. The foundation is very helpful and offers maps of its trails. The telephone is (203) 355-3715.

Down Route 7 on the east side one mile north of the Brookfield line is the Candlewood Country Club, open all year except that you can't play golf between December and April. It has a pro shop, tennis court and a restaurant. The club is privately owned but open to the public. The manager is Beth Ford and the number is (203) 354-9354.

Lying along the western border of Litchfield County and partly in Fairfield is big Candlewood Lake. Sixty years ago, when it was created, no one foresaw that it would be the largest and one of the most beautiful lakes in Connecticut, a priceless resource and summer haven for people from all over for swimming, boating, and fishing. Would you believe an 11-pound trout?

There are launching ramps up and down Candlewood's shores, also a number of marinas, some of which are Chatterton Marine in New Fairfield, (203) 746-9138; Boatland in Brookfield, (203) 775-4549; Causeway Marine in New Fairfield, (203) 746-2100; Brookfield Bay Marina and Yacht Club, (203) 740-2628; Marineland in New Milford, (203) 354-3929; Pocono Marina in Danbury, (203) 743-9572; and Candlewood East Sailing Center in Brookfield, (203) 775-2253.

There are three tackle and bait shops: Hank's Tackle Shop

SUNNY VALLEY, NEW MILFORI

CANDLEWOOD LAKE

on Germantown Road in Danbury, (203) 743-2221; The
Valley Angler on Padanarun Road in New Fairfield, (203)
792-8324; and Bill's Bait and Tackle, 348 Danbury Road in
New Milford, (203) 354-9066.

The Candlewood Lake Authority is there to answer your
questions, so call Frances Frattini, a kind, helpful, and authori-
tative lady. Her number is (203) 354-6928.

You will find your trip to Candlewood Lake a delight any
season.

Continuing your adventure, keep going up Route 7 and
when you get to where Route 37 branches off, there is a must
stop. Voltaire's Shop and Gallery is a place full of contemporary,
hand-crafted items in stoneware, wood, clay, crystal, and glass.
It's a wonderful store, unique, not just a gift shop. The things
it sells are works of art for use in everyday living, not just
attractive merchandise. Every place you look you see something
beautiful.

Its owners are Alice Voltaire and her husband, John Seymour.
Alice and he late husband, Paul Voltaire, a Viennese jeweler,
sculptor, and inventor, created the place 26 years ago. John
Seymour is a superlative craftsman, his specialty being animals.
His bears and other beasts are so beguiling that if they weren't
stone, you'd cuddle them.

A spell of browsing at Voltaire's will set fire to your imagination. You won't want to leave, The number is (203) 354-4200.

The next town north of New Milford, after you have whizzed
past condos, real estate offices, shopping malls, and a potpourri
of you name it, is Gaylordsville. It's not very big, but it's got
some things in it that are worth your digging out.

Before you gèt into town, a road goes left, called Gaylordsville
Road. It's a pretty road with pleasant sights of farm land. Soon
you will come to an enormous oak tree with a sign hanging on
it that tells you that George Washington stopped here one day
in 1780 to have his lunch and confer with his generals. They

OLD SCHOOLHOUSE, GAYLORDSVILLE

included Lafayette. Not far beyond is a little red school house on the right. It's a quaint sight. When you enter you will be in what is said to be the last one-room school in Connecticut. It was opened 227 years ago. It is carefully preserved, exactly as it was on the day in 1967 when the last class was dismissed. Pictures of classes going back many years are on the walls, and the teacher's desk is still there with school books of long ago. It is open in August and September from 2 to 4 in the afternoon.

Gaylordsville is a post office, store, fire house, basket weaving shop, and not much else. But two doors south of the post office is Rocky's River Cafe, a good little place with good food, open all day.

The next road after Rocky's will take you to the Merwinsville Hotel Restoration. Don't miss it. Barbara Thorland and a committee have been restoring the old building for many months. Years ago trains stopped here long enough for passengers to get off and grab a bite. Everything went along fine until the railroad added dining cars to the trains.

The ticket office is still there and the freight office. When you step into the parlor of the little hotel you will be back in the Victorian era. Upstairs are bedrooms and a lounge and on the third floor is a ballroom that runs the length of the building. A latticed balcony looks out over the tracks. A visit to Merwinsville is total nostalgia.

Up the road is Brown's Forge, left exactly as it was when the surviving Brown brother stopped work on a day after World War II ended. It has to be the only forge of its kind. Two Brown brothers had forges side by side. One was a blacksmith, who made iron tires for wagon wheels, hinges, plows and tools, anything of iron. The other shod horses and oxen. On one side of the room is a contrivance that swings out from the wall when needed to restrain beasts difficult to shoe, especially oxen. The ox was jacked up off the floor in a truss around his middle. His protests got him no place. If you are interested in ancient

MORNING TRAIN

implements and would like to poke around in an old forge, this place is for you, but you can only go on Sundays in August. The man who explains the place to you will probably be Alan Dodd. The shop operated until 1962.

Just north of the bridge on Route 7 on the left is The Basket Shop, run by Ruth and Carol Hotchkiss. Its specialty is baskets, from thumb-sized to huge We didn't see any balloon baskets, but if you wanted one, we venture the Hotchkisses would get you one. The shop sells other things, glassware, postcards, toys, brass items, jewelry, cotton afghans, preserves and ice cream. Quite a place. The number is (203) 354-6202.

No one coming up Route 7 past Bull's Ridge would have the slightest notion that the Housatonic River would transform itself from a lazy river into a wild confusion of cascades that explode over their dams and tumble down in noisy frothy beauty.

Bull's Ridge is north of Gaylordsville. A traffic light and not much else is all you find there except the very attractive Bull's Bridge Inn which says of itself, "Country Fare with European Flair." It has spacious, pleasant dining rooms and excellent cuisine. The number is (203) 927-3263.

At the light, turn left, go down a slope and over a little covered bridge. We hope you go after a big rain because of the heightened drama of the crashing falls. You'll soon hear the roar and get your camera out. To the right are paths that take you beside the river and through the woods. There are several places where you can get gorgeous pictures from high, steep banks, so be careful. The current is swift and if you fall in you'll soon be on your way to New Milford. The path goes north about half a mile. There is another bridge on this road. Cross it and park on the left. A lane south along the river will take you back to Gaylordsville.

After you have taken your pictures of the Bull's Bridge cascades, continue west and take the next road right. This is

SHOD AND READY TO GO, GAYLORDSVILLE

BULL'S BRIDGE, KENT

Schaghticoke Road and will take you to Kent on a little used narrow road along the Housatonic. It's a very pretty drive. After a while you will come to houses. This is the Schaghticoke Indian Reservation, the remnant of a once large tribe, people who go about their business of making a living. Some distance beyond

the houses is their ancient burying ground, a level area with a
hill rising steeply behind it. It is enclosed in a fence and the
gravestones are in a neat, long row. The largest is at one end. It
is inscribed, "Eunice Mauwee, a Christian Indian, 1756-1860."

Soon you will come to the big, well-known Kent School.
When you get to Route 341, turn left. Before we take you into
Kent, we would like you to visit the trails of Pond Mountain
and Fuller Road, a lovely area with delightful walks and beautiful views.

Turn left on Route 341, right on Macedonia Brook Road,
and take another right on Fuller Mountain Road, then go a short
distance to a parking place. A walk around Fuller Pond is very
pleasant, so are all the trails that branch off. The trail marked
"Mountain Pond" is spectacular. There ia a place in the parking
area where you can leave your name and pick up a map of the
area. On the other side of Fuller Pond is Fuller Mountain Road,
where the Appalachian Trail goes along for a way, then branches
off and takes you to Caleb's Peak and another peak, designed
only for people who like airy heights and beautiful views and
don't mind tough going. Keep going and soon the trail will lead
you to St. John's Ledges, sheer cliffs meant only for mountain
goats and intrepid rockclimbers.

Macedonia Brook Road will take you into the state park
campground. A winding road takes you to the office where you
can register, pick your campsite, read all the scoop, and be about
your business of having a good time.

Now, after finishing this sojourn, please return to Route 341
and head east into the ancient and very interesting town of Kent.

Cross Route 7 at the traffic light, go over the railroad tracks
to a red barn and white silo where Karen Chase's Kent Farm
and Garden Center is. Karen says that hers is the only feed store
in northwest Connecticut and that she can feed animals from
mouse to elephant. Karen provides advice on animal nutrition
and first aid. Her number is (203) 927-4146.

HOUSATONIC AT BULL'S BRIDGE

Go back to the monument and traffic light in the middle of Route 7 and you will be looking up the wide main street of a lovely, old and very much alive New England town. The street is lined with handsome houses, once private residences, now commercial buildings.

The House of Books on the right shares its ground floor with the Kent Bridge Gallery, and upstairs next door is an equally highly regarded gallery, the Bachelier-Cardonsky, which the *New York Times* paid tribute to. The *Times* also commends a nearby gallery in a railroad car, run by Jacques Kaplan.

The new Kent Town Center on your left as you go north is a congeries of shops, among which is Folkcraft Instruments, an outlet for dulcimers, folk harps, psalteries, books, records, tapes, and other things to supply the needs of folk musicians. The telephone number is (203) 927-4492.

Nancy Murello's Rose Gallery in the old railroad station encourages young artists to exhibit work that reaches out to people and enriches their lives. The big collection is stimulating. You will see several marbles of a sculptor of promise, Edward Alpi, whose imagination soars. The Rose Gallery's number is (203) 927-4772.

South of the traffic light is a fine little restaurant, the Milk Pail, and farther south is the well-stocked Kent Greenhouse.

A few stores up from the House of Books is a popular restaurant called the Villager. Behind it is the big Kent Commons, with a spread of shops that covers acres.

Across Route 7 from the railroad station is a much sought-after restaurant and inn, the Fife 'n Drum, and on the north side of its parking lot is the Fife 'n Drum gift shop with a large selection of things. The number for the restaurant and inn is (203) 927-3618.

North of Kent Commons and on the same side is an attractive bed and breakfast run by Alan and Brenda Hodgson, a British couple who call their place Chaucer House because they come from Canterbury, where Geoffrey Chaucer wrote his famous tales.

Now we've pretty well hit the high spots in the central part of Kent, so let us go speeding up Route 7 for about three miles to the ancient part of Kent, Flanders District. That was where the action was until the railroad came and everything went south with it, almost. No one knows why Flanders.

At the curve in the road on the left is a perfectly beautiful old house, large and patrician, now a fine bed and breakfast, called Flander Arms, owned and run by an attractive couple, Marc and Marilyn DeVos. The house dates from 1738 and is set in wide lawns among huge trees. It is on the National Register of Historic Places.

The DeVos' taste in furniture and decoration is impeccable. The number is (203) 927-3040; open only by reservation.

Across the road is one of Kent's prizes, Seven Hearths, the home and studio of one of America's fine and most prolific artists, George Laurence Nelson. The house was unusual for its time because of its size. It's big and three-storied with nine-foot ceilings, ideal for the purposes the Kent Historical Society, its owner, puts it to. It is used mostly for the display of Nelson's work. His output was prodigious: portraits, landscapes here and in France, watercolors, oils, drawings. It took several years for the original owner, John Beebe, Jr., to build his house. He finished it in 1754.

Laurence and Helen Nelson were warm and friendly people who contributed much to the life and times of Kent. Seven Hearths is a treasure. We strongly urge you not to miss a chance to visit it. It is open on Saturdays and Sundays in July and August, from 2 to 4:30. Miss Emily Hopson, a gracious, obliging, and knowledgeable lady, is the person to call for information about the Nelson House. Her number is (203) 927-3419.

Up Route 7 on the left is what we certainly want you not to miss, the Sloane Stanley Museum, the combined genius of Eric

Sloane and Donald Davis, president of the famed Stanley Works. Eric Sloane could aptly be described as "Mr. America." His warm-hearted, engaging personality shines throughout his work.

He painted rural America as no one has ever done, its church spires, cloud formations, covered bridges, and railroad stations. His largest work is in the lobby of the National Air and Space Museum in Washington. It is seven stories high and half a city block long.

Sloane developed a deep interest in early American tools, and he and Davis hatched the idea of a museum to display them. It's certainly some display. There you will see an enormous collection of the implements our pioneers ancestors fashioned and used to hew their lives out of the wilderness of colonial America.

So, go over the railroad tracks and into a pretty little green with the unassuming museum on your right. An agreeable lady will welcome you and point you to the big room where you will be awash in Mr. Sloane's remarkable collection. All these things were born of stark necessity. They are beautiful because their honest use made them so.

Eric Sloane's studio and workshop are there in the museum, re-created from his home in nearby Warren. It's a big, homey room with everything in the world in it he needed in his career as an artist, writer and craftsman. He wrote more than 30 books.

On the grounds is a replica of the house the pioneers lived in, a small, dark building with tiny windows and an earth floor, a bed with rope for a mattress, a chair or two, homemade of course, a dresser and not much else.

Near the little house is what's left of the forge the settlers used to fashion the tools you saw inside. If you have any feeling for what our ancestors went through to give us the wonderful country we live in today, you won't soon forget your visit to Mr.

GEORGE LAURENCE NELSON HOUSE, KENT

Sloane's museum. Eric Sloane is buried under a huge maple outside the museum.

The museum is open Wednesday through Sunday, 10 to 4:30, mid-May through October. The number is (203) 927-3849.

Further up Route 7, also on the left, is a big, charming old

TEA AT THE NELSON HOUSE, KENT

house that is the Country Goose, beautiful and spotlessly maintained by it owner, Phyllis Dietrich, as a bed and breakfast. The house is a delight inside with Phyllis's artistic and winsome touches. An inviting atmosphere will greet you with the aroma of baking and the sight of a well-filled library. The house dates

ERIC SLOANE

from 1740 and was recently renovated by Phyllis and her husband. The telephone is (203) 927-4746.

Not far north of the Country Goose is a small, unusual and popular store called Kenko Natural Grocery, owned and run by Naoko Robinson and Leonard Urbanowicz. Unusual because its specialty is organically raised vegetables and holistic food,

SLOANE-STANLEY MUSEUM, KENT

seeds, grains, fruits, vitamins, macrobiotic food, tofu, and rice, the store sells books and has a deli. The telephone is (203) 927-4079.

One more delight before we head north on the second tour. Several miles up the road is the Kent Falls State Park, one of the most attractive spots in the county. On one side of the little park is the drama of the falls that come crashing down on wide stone steps to froth into a brook that's big enough to splash and tumble in. Even in the dryness of mid-summer the falls are lovely. After a heavy rain they're sensational.

There is a green in the park big enough for a ball game. There are picnic tables, privies, and drinking fountains. A path with log steps goes up to a bridge from which you can lean over and watch the falls rushing beneath you.

KENT FALLS

SECOND TOUR

The second tour starts at Cornwall Bridge, turns west over Ellsworth Hill to Sharon, it goes through Lakeville and Salisbury to Canaan, then to Falls Village and Lime Rock, and finally it goes south to West Cornwall and Cornwall.

THE FIRST THING YOU SEE WHEN YOU GO DOWN THE HILL into Cornwall Bridge is the sign of Todd Piker's pottery. Todd is a prominent potter and this is where he works his magic with clay. His showroom and warehouse are here. His retail store is in West Cornwall and we'll tell you more about him when we get there.

Beyond the pottery is the Hitching Post Motel, whose number is (203) 672-6219, and Baird's General Store for groceries, sandwiches, coffee and gossip.

Across the street is the big and well-stocked hardware store, Northwest Lumber, with helpful people to wait on you. Next to it is the New England Catering and Food Company, run by Susan Kochman and Eileen Reichert. The things these enterprising ladies serve on the spot and to go have earned them an enviable reputation. Their shelves are filled with all kinds of food, exotic and ordinary. Their number is (203) 672-6554.

The shops here include a video rental, a vet, an antique shop and the old established Housatonic Valley Rug Shop, whose owner is Gerald Blakey. The shop supplies rugs and carpets to a wide area. Beyond these places are the post office, the Cornwall Bridge Package Store and the National Iron Bank.

Across the bridge is a gas station and Nora's Nursery, run by kind and efficient ladies.

There is a place we must tell you about that you get to by curving around under the bridge and heading south on the road along the river. A mile later is a white house that says "Milkhouse Pottery." It is a shop of an accomplished potter, Susan Fox, who extensively shows her line of every imaginable kind of pot. Susan is a hard worker, at her potter's wheel by the hour crafting beautiful pieces of her own design. She is widely respected for her unusual work and has a loyal following. She gives lessons. Her number is (203) 672-6450, and she likes to be called first.

Down the road past Susan's place are lovely walks and picnic spots along the river.

Now we head west to Sharon, 12 miles away. Almost at once on the right is an unusual enterprise, a greenhouse that wholesales edible flowers for a growing demand. The owners are Alan and Marcia Lawrance. Their number is (203) 672-6757.

The road to Sharon is lovely because it lies on a wide plane with the countryside spread out before you in all directions. At the top of a long hill is Ellsworth Hill Farm where you can pick berries in season and the shop is a fine farm store with pleasant smells of apples and other things. The telephone is (203) 364-0249.

Before you get into Sharon is a treat, especially if you have children, but even if you haven't. It is the Sharon Audubon Center, once the home of Mr. and Mrs. Clement R. Ford. It is now an active vital treasure owned by the National Audubon Society with a commodious house set on 684 acres with 12 miles of trails to wander through the wildlife all around you. The whole place is a learning center, an eye-opener for people of all ages. The big house is offices and lecture rooms, living quarters for young interns, an extensive library, and a book shop.

There are cages with turtles in them and an infirmary for injured birds. In one of them, an injured barn owl sulks in the back of his cage, looking darkly at the world.

There aren't many Audubon centers around the country. The one in Sharon is one of the best. The place is a beehive of activity, with introductory ecology for wee explorers, hiking, crafts, games, and the freedom to explore the gardens and trails. The telephone is (203) 364-0520.

Your first sight as you go down the hill into Sharon is of the big stone clock tower, a landmark since 1884, that stands sentinel between a wide avenue of handsome mansions and the village green, truly a breath-taking sight, deserving of its title, "One of America's masterpieces." Once shaded by mighty elms, it prompted Thoreau to say, "Such an avenue of elms...thronging over streets with witchery, brushing farmhouse gables with their wings...a picture and a poem."

An old and beautiful house on the north side of the green is the Gay-Hoyt House, home of the Sharon Historical Society and a museum of fascinating collections of antique furniture and clothing, paintings, old calf bindings, and other treasures. The society hums with activity and invites you to share in its programs. The telephone is (203) 364-5688.

A little north of the town is a traffic light, and on that corner on the left is a large and handsome house which the owner, Carole Tangen, calls "1890 Colonial." The house is beautifully furnished and maintained. It is a first class bed and breakfast. The number is (203) 364-0436, and if that doesn't answer, call (203) 364-3585.

Now we leave this lovely town of colonial antiquity and head north to Lakeville. The views on the way are beautiful, especially over your left shoulder.

At the traffic circle are the buildings of the well-known college preparatory school, Hotchkiss, and down on the left is the Interlaken Inn and Restaurant with 80 guest rooms and facilities for conventions, sports, fitness, and other activities. The number is (203) 435-9878. Back on Route 41 a short way beyond Hotchkiss is Woodlands, a fine little restaurant, whose number is (203) 435-0578. Not far down the road is the Wake Robin Inn, a restored, handsome old inn with 40 guest rooms, a swimming pool and attractive grounds. The telephone is (203) 435-2515.

Lakeville is a pretty little town despite its being cut in two by a major highway. Traffic is just something the people who live there now have to endure. On your left as you approach is a lake with a name as long as it is, Wonomskopomuc. It's for residents only.

Iron mines were once the big thing in Lakeville. The mines here and in Salisbury won for the region the name "Arsenal of the Revolution," because it was here that General Washington's cannons and cannonballs and other implements of war came from.

Now, down the hill into Lakeville. Before you get to the blinker, turn left up a rise, and there is a neat little restaurant, the Brothers, whose number is (203) 435-9466. Across the way is the old railroad station, and beyond it is what once was the Holley Manufacturing Company that made superior knives. It is now a fine restaurant called Holley Place. The area is appropriately called Pocketknife Square. The phone is (203) 435-2727.

Another treat in this ancient town is up on Main Street, the Holley-Williams House, a treasure owned by the Salisbury Association. It was built in 1808 and lived in by five generations of the Holley family. Its stately, columned porch and fanlight doorway are shown off to good advantage by its position above the street. The furniture and decoration seem to hark back to more than a century ago.

HOLLEY-WILLIAMS HOUSE, LAKEVILLE

The relics you will see include an enormous, carefully mounted collection of knives and the set of china designed for Governor Alexander Hamilton Holley's inaugural ball. Call (203) 435-2878 before you go.

Golden China, a good Chinese restaurant, is on Main Street at the blinker. Do drive through Main Street slowly. It's wide and lined with handsome old houses. One of the side streets will take you to the *Lakeville Journal*, an old and respected paper that serves a community that includes towns in Massachusetts and New York.

On your left behind a handsome fence is an equally handsome house, Burton Brook Farm, whose owners are Virginia and Marvin Rosen. Their house is large and perfectly suited to the display of their treasures, rare and beautiful oriental art and antique jewelry. (The jewelry can be seen only by appointment.)

When you go in the door you will think you are entering someone's private house, so organized and uncluttered it is.

If you have a yen for oriental art, gorgeous vases that look as if they should be in museums, little carved ivory chessmen and other lovely things, this is the place you should browse. The Rosens have a remarkable collection of prints called "botanicals." Their number is (203) 435-9241.

Across the street is a small shopping center worth cruising through. Lakeville runs right into Salisbury, both of which are ancient New England towns, the likes of which it would be hard to find. The stone building on your right is the Scoville Memorial Library, whose collections are as complete and interesting as far-sighted librarians and trustees can make them. Across the street is the distinguished Bushnell Tavern, a coach stop in colonial times, now privately owned.

Several blocks beyond the Bushnell is Academy Street to the right. On it are a fine big market and the Lion's Head book shop, and a small select store called Harris Foods, which "prepares fresh, seasonal foods for any occasion, blending flavor with imagination." Its telephone is (203) 435-2062.

Beside the tavern is Selleck Hill Road, and if you feel like a little diversion, take the left fork and go to the top of the hill for really lovely views. The right fork takes you through the woods on a little jaunt that is dealt with on the first tour of *Exploring the Berkshires.*

Across the street from the tavern is a centuries-old marker that says, "164 1/2 miles to Boston." Beyond it is the handsome town hall. It resembles one that was burned down some years ago by an arsonist. The Ragamont Inn, a small but fine hotel with an excellent restaurant, is across the street, and beside it is the Three Ravens Antiques Shop whose owners, the Harold Corbins, are discerning collectors.

At the fork that joins Route 41 and Route 44 is the ancient and beautiful White Hart Inn, one of Salisbury's prideful places, a fine, year-round hotel, newly renovated, freshly decorated, its cuisine excellent, everything about it first-class. The telephone is (203) 435-0030.

If you like the thought of a small and attractive bed and breakfast, you'll find one a few doors up from the White Hart on the same side, at Yesterday's Yankee. The house is a Cape Cod cottage dating from 1744. It serves substantial and yummy breakfasts. The number is (203) 435-9539, and the owners are Doris and Dick Alexander.

Continue on Route 44 past the twin lakes with the sad story of poor Indian girls. We would like you to take Vaughn Gray's map to guide you around and between these. The first one you come to is Lake Washinee, which means "Smiling Water," and the other larger one is Lake Washining, "Laughing Water." There is no public swimming in either lake.

The legend is about two sisters who lived a pleasant life by their two lakes until one day came when a young brave from another tribe was captured and marked for torture. The girls

WHITE HART INN, SALISBURY

took one look at him and fell for him. They hurried to their father, the chief, and pleaded for the young man's life. Nothing doing. This set the girls off into spasms of grief, a grief so intense they climbed into their canoe and paddled out onto the water. They were never seen again. Some misty, moonlit night, if you are consumed with curiosity, go down to the shore of Lake Washining and you just might see an empty canoe floating out there. Maybe you won't.

Along the shore of Lake Washining is O'Hara's Landing Marina where you can hire or buy boats, get bait, tackle and ice, and eat. The large, full-service establishment is the only public access to the lakes. There is a channel joining the two lakes, but the clearance under the bridge is only three feet.

The owner of the marina is David Haab. His number is (203) 824-7583. David reports that the prize catch in Connecticut was a 17-pound brown trout caught in one of the twin lakes. He also said that Kikanee salmon, which reproduce here naturally, abound in the lakes. David's marina is open from the third Saturday in April to a date in February that is fixed each year.

On the way to Canaan is an appealing and useful little operation called Sweethaven Farm, owned and run by Noreen Driscoll, whose wealth of knowledge about herbs and flowers marks her place as a mecca for people who want to buy herbs for artistic and culinary purposes.

Noreen farms her eight acres organically and raises hundreds of varieties of herbs and flowers which she dries in her barn and does charming things with: everlasting herbal wreaths, custom-designed arrangements, fragrant potpourris, gift baskets, topiaries and other delights.

Noreen holds craft workshops where you may take lessons in working with herbs and flowers. She keeps her classes small, so call before you go. Her number is (203) 824-5764. Take Route 44 east towards Canaan and turn left on Twin Lakes Road, then right on Weatogue Road. Sweethaven Farm is on the left.

In the center of town is the railroad station, built in 1872 and so handsome and historic that it is on the National Register of Historic Places. There is a restaurant in the station and another nearby called the Cannery, owned and run by Diane and Eric Stephens, that has been selected by the *New York Times* restaurant reviewer for her year-end list of best restaurants in Connecticut.

The Housatonic Railroad runs excursion trains between Canaan and Cornwall Bridge. For schedules, call (203) 824-0339.

Canaan isn't exactly a fascination for visitors, but there are

SUMMER IN THE LITCHFIELD HILLS

several things we'd like you to see. East on Route 44 is the best preserved iron furnace in the whole area. There are others, but they are on private property. This one is owned by the state. When you get to the North Canaan Congregational church, turn in and go past it. It is set back from the road and is very pretty. Follow the Lower River Road around to the right until you come to a steep, short driveway on your left. It leads directly down to the Beckley furnace on the shore of the Blackberry River with its scenic falls. It's a good little diversion, a quiet spot for a picnic with the old relic and the river flowing by to photograh.

East of the church you just passed is Lone Oak, the largest private campground in Connecticut with every facility for your comfort and pleasure. The number to call for reservations is (203) 824-7051, or toll free, 1-800-422-CAMP.

Now go back to Canaan, go left at the traffic light on Route 63, follow the road around a curve and go right, which will take you to Falls Village. It's not very big so poke around until you hit Main Street. There is the imposing Hunt Library, very interesting architecturally and very good. On the same side is River Running Expeditions, as complete an establishment as you will find anywhere to cater to people who want to canoe or kayak on the Housatonic. Their shop is stocked with all your needs. They will take you to the Falls Village Power Plant and launch you on a wonderful 12-mile trip down the river to Cornwall Bridge and arrange for you to camp overnight at the Housatonic Meadows campground.

If white water gives you butterflies in your tummy, they will take you to Ashley Falls for a 14-mile adventure of the sleepy Housatonic around Bartholomew's Cobble through its bird sanctuary.

So put yourselves in Joan Manasse's capable hands and she and her crew will tailor-make the expedition that is just to your taste. Her number is (203)824-5579.

CANAAN UNION STATION

The Pease Library on the main street of Canaan satisfies the needs of the town, and upstairs is a natural history museum whose scope is beyond what you would expect to find in a town of Canaan's size. The collection is impressive, from tiny songbirds to eagles. Most of the birds and animals come from the

CHURCH IN NORTH CANAAN

environs of Canaan, some from far places. The library's telephone is (203) 824-7863.

Down the street on the left is the Falls Village-Canaan
Historical Society Museum, a little gem that will take you back
a century or two and beguile you with ancient documents and
books, maps, postcards of long ago, signs, old bottles, a model
railroad engine, a dressmaker's dummy with a World War I Red
Cross woman in her uniform, a merry-go-round horse so old he
ought to be put out to grass, and a tiny telephone switchboard
with a skinny little old female operator sitting in front of it.

The nearest telephone is in the town clerk's office in the same
building. It is (203) 824-0707. The museum is open only on
Friday, year-round, from 2 to 4:40.

Around the corner is the Cornerstone Gallery of Fine Arts, a
working studio with classes and exhibits of the members' work.
It's a good place with a lot going on. To find out what, call (203)
824-0390.

Across the street is The Inn, a very fine restaurant owned by
Patrick and Janice Hibbits. It's open every day from 3 to 9, and
Saturdays and Sundays for lunch. The number is (203) 824-
7148. Down the street from The Inn is a short curving drive
under the railroad bridge and to the right where there are the
complexes of the Connecticut Light and Power Company's
plant with its turbines, canals, and huge dam. Sometimes water
goes roaring over it and sometimes nothing, depending upon
the need for power. Go past the big building and over the bridge.
Turn right and you will find yourselves in a quiet parking area
on the river with a walk into the woods at its far end. If you
come upon bushes with red berries, don't eat the berries.

A left turn over the bridge will bring you to a larger parking
area with a good view of the dam.

Up Route 7 a short way is the Village Coffee Shop, open
Monday through Friday. For hours call (203) 824-7886. There
are cabins for rent behind the restaurant.

FALLS VILLAGE A CENTURY AGO

HOUSATONIC VALLEY REGIONAL HIGH SCHOOL & TOURIST TRAIN

Go south a little way on Route 126 and take a swing to the right past the big, vital Housatonic Valley Regional High School to Lime Rock Park, the oldest automobile race track in continuous use in the United States. It is the road racing center of the East, a lovely setting in a valley with hills all around and green fields. There are car races there from spring until fall. The number to call to find out when is (203) 435-2571. Sandwiched in between public races are car club events. For information about these clubs, call the same number. Lime Rock Park is big, colorful, noisy, and exciting, a great place to get rid of your hang-ups.

A sign on the right across from the high school will direct you to Music Mountain and the oldest summer chamber music center in the United States, founded by Jacques Gordon 60 years ago. On weekends all summer long there are concerts by the world's famous string and wind ensembles. If you like chamber music, a Sunday afternoon on Music Mountain is a lovely place to be listening to the best music in the world played by the best musicians with the big doors open to the view of far away mountains. For tickets and information call (203) 496-1222.

Flowing swiftly along Route 7, the Housatonic River is sometimes turbulent, sometimes peaceful. On your right is Clarke Outdoors, an establishment for outdoors people, mostly canoers and kayakers. It's owned and run by Mark Clarke, a National Open Canoe champion, and his wife, Jenifer. They have a huge inventory of canoes, kayaks, paddles, jackets, dry suits, car racks, clothes, books, and anything else you might need for your sport, and if they haven't got what you want, they'll get it for you.

An expert staff will give you lessons, take you up to Falls Village, and after telling you everything you should know, they will launch you on a 10-mile trip down the river and pick you up in the afternoon, take you back to their place, and give you lunch.

It's a wonderful way to spend a day, and you don't have to be a hot-shot canoeist. The Clarkes' number is (203) 672-6365.

On the west side of Route 7 are two camping areas a mile or so apart. The numbers to call to make arrangements to camp there are (203) 672-6772 for the campground; the park office is (203) 927-3238.

Soon on the right is the entrance to the Pine Knob Loop, a hiking trail on the blue blaze system.

A mile or so on the left side of the road is a wide and inviting area with a sign saying, "Housatonic Meadows State Park." Up

HUNT LIBRARY, FALLS VILLAGE

and down the park are picnic tables and pleasant drives through the woods, mostly pines. There is a launching ramp for small boats, privies, drinking water, places where you can swim and fish. Across the road are buildings where you can get bait and flies, and whatever else you may need.

If you need more help, call the Department of Environmental Protection, Bureau of State Parks and Forests, 165 Capitol Avenue, Hartford, (203) 566-2304.

We are now at Cornwall Bridge with our next stop West Cornwall. To get there, head east over the big bridge on Route 4. In about four miles you will come to a crossroads. Turn left on Route 125 and in a few minutes, look for a sign on the left that says, "Dibble Hill Road." Head in, and when you come to a sign, "The Hilltop," you've reached one of the highest points in Cornwall, and a beguiling bed and breakfast run by Everett VanDorn. The place is so secluded that the only sounds you are likely to hear will be the wind sighing in the trees, or maybe an owl. You will be well and comfortably cared for, and the views of faraway mountains are spectacular. Everett's number is (203) 672-6871.

Now, back to Route 125 and down the winding road into West Cornwall, a beguiling little town, different from any in the region. On your left is a big gray building that houses the 50,000-book collection of Barbara Farnsworth, a specialist not only in general stock, but also art, horticulture, and fine printing. Mrs. Farnsworth is an appraiser. Her hours are usually Saturday from 9 to 5, or by appointment. Her number is (203) 672-6571.

Across the street is Yutzler's, a long-established food store. Down a little way on the corner is the Cornwall Bridge Pottery Store, an inviting place owned and run by Todd Piker and his wife. Todd's pottery, as we have mentioned on the way up Route 7, is in Cornwall Bridge, but here in West Cornwall is

HOUSATONIC RIVER

his large retail establishment, the shop of a world-renowned potter with a generation of experience behind him.

Years ago, Piker supplied the table settings for a White House luncheon. By invitation, he has exhibited his wares at the Los Angeles Folk Craft Museum, the Indianapolis Museum of Art, and other places. You will find leather goods and other things in the shop. The telephone is (203) 672-6545.

The old railroad station is right there on the summer excursion route. In it is the Little Benefit Shop, where you will find an appealing assortment of things. The "benefit" is the Little Guild of St. Francis, a well-run shelter nearby for stray dogs and cats.

The Covered Bridge Cafe is a step from the station. Across the street is Freshfields, an elegant top-drawer restaurant, whose number is (203) 672-6601.

Around the corner on River Road is an embarrassment of riches, two antique shops. The first one you come to is that of Michael D. Trapp, whose flair is statuary, old books, old furniture, glass, lamps, pewter, old signs, old silver, old jewelry. His number is (203) 672-6098.

Next door are David and Karen Mason, antiquarians of long experience, knowledgeable and pleasant, whose large house is filled with intriguing things that should be in museums, enormous and beautiful vases, lovely pieces of oriental art. Their number is (203) 672-6274.

Past the two shops is an appealing little road that winds along the river, an ideal place for a nice walk.

Not very far is a sign that says, "Deborah Benson, Bookseller." It is the establishment of a lady who specializes in books on early medicine, modern firsts, *Alice in Wonderland*, and other subjects. She is an appraiser and will conduct search. She will see you only be appointment at (203) 672-6614.

Next to Freshfields is an attractive little bed and breakfast, Mill Brook House, run by Mary Gilroy. Across the street is the

MOHAWK MT. SKI AREA, CORNWALL

quaint little shop Mary also runs, called Vintage Clothing. If you want the kind of clothing worn from 1850 to 1950, Mary's shop is the place to go. Her two establishments are open all year, and the number is (203) 672-6163.

Almost next door is a tiny, cozy restaurant called Cadwell's

GATHERING MAPLE SAP FOR SUGARING

CATHEDRAL PINES IN CORNWALL
BEFORE THE HURRICANE OF 1989

Corner, where you can get breakfast and lunch. The number is (203) 672-0101.

Across the street is the shop of Ian Ingersoll, a famous cabinet maker, where you will find tables and chairs and other attractive pieces of furniture, all beautifully made to Quaker design. Ian's telephone is (203) 672-6334.

At the end of the street in this charming little village is the ancient covered bridge, a fine, sturdy old structure that has withstood floods and gales since 1864.

Before we end this second tour, we have several diversions. The first is to the famous Mohawk Ski Area in Cornwall. To get there, go east out of West Cornwall four miles to the blinker on Route 4. A short way to the right is the sign directing you to the area. Soon, there it is on your left, with the vast slopes in the background and in the foreground, the lodge where you can rent skis and boots and whatever else you need. The area has snow-making equipment and also night skiing. The telephone is (203) 672-6464.

Secluded deep in the woods is a place where there is a pond and boat launch and a good spot for picnics. Continue on the road past the ski area and take the next left on Great Hill Road, and another left at a Camp Mohawk sign. A sign to Mohawk Pond will bring you to it. There is a parking area and a privy. Fishing is spotty, we are told.

Now back to the blinkers at the four corners, and go right. At the top of a long hill, go right to a sign into the Mohawk State Forest, the other attraction in Cornwall. It's a huge place with hiking trails, picnic tables, and an observation tower for fabulous views.

If you have a love for plants and would like to see rare species, go to the forest ranger's headquarters, park, and look for a sign to the Black Spruce Bog. A footpath will lead you to a boardwalk into the bog. Stay on the boardwalk because the plant life is too delicate to be trampled on.

SKIER

MOHAWK MT. SKI AREA

FARM IN WEST CORNWALL
from a photo by Pam Reagan

The bog was formed by an enormous block of glacial ice that made a hole 40 feet deep. Water, then plant life, gradually filled the hole from the edge to the center. The bog is a wet area of about two acres where black spruces, larches, and white pines grow. Plants you will find there include creeping snowberry, sphagnum moss, wild calla, and sedge.

To get to two more places we'd like you to see, go back to Route 4, to Cornwall Bridge, and head south. Go up Route 45 for several miles until you get to Turning Point Farm on your right. Evelyn and Joseph Grossi have turned their 250-year-old house into an enchantingly decorated bed and breakfast. The guest rooms are large and comfortable, and the view over fields and woods is the kind that draws you to the window. The telephone is (203) 868-7775.

The last thing on this tour is the attractive and popular Cornwall Inn, down Route 7 not far on the right. It is a small motel with an excellent restaurant. In the summer you dine under a large awning on a wide terrace looking out over flower gardens and a pool.

That's it for the second tour, and we hope you enjoyed it.

LUTHERAN CHURCH, CORNWALL

THIRD TOUR

The third tour starts in New Milford, makes a long swing up Route 202 to New Preston, circles around Lake Waramaug, then backtracks to Bantam and Litchfield.

WE'VE DONE NEW MILFORD, SO HEAD NORTH ON ROUTE 202. Five miles later, turn right on Upland Road and you'll come to the Silo, a must stop on these tours. It would be hard to miss this group of fine looking farm buildings: two federal houses, big barns, sheds. and two silos.

For years Ruth and Skitch Henderson had wanted a place in the country and they found what they were looking for, 200 acres of beautiful rolling farm land five miles north of New Milford off Upland Road on the right, a place with two houses, barns, and silos. Soon the Hendersons' dynamo got cranked up and their creation became the Silo. It is now an internationally acclaimed cooking school that attracts the world's great chefs to go there and teach. The classes are large and the students get to chop, stir, and taste. It's a fun operation and very popular.

The staff at the Silo is devoted and experienced. They run the cooking school, the food, housewares and book shops. And everything else that goes on in this fascinating and sophisticated establishment.

After you have prowled around this enchanting place, go back

Route 202 and head north. Turn left on Route 45 and you will be in New Preston, a little village with a rich concentration of shops and galleries, meat and drink for the antiques hunter. Hunting for antiques is pretty much what New Preston is all about.

There are antique dealers on both sides of the street and several book dealers with their interesting specialties.

Behind the shops on Main Street is a place for poets, a photogenic little waterfall and a brook that burbles and sings. The road that passes Tim Mawson's book shop crosses the brook and winds up the hill past a very pretty stone church and on through beautiful country. It's a rewarding drive and will take you back to Kent or to Lake Waramaug. Very pleasant.

The road past New Preston, Route 45, flows around the east end of Lake Waramaug. Soon, Doc's Restaurant is on your right, a good little place with delicious food. Doc's telephone is (203)868-9415. Around a curve in the lake is the famed Boulders Inn overlooking Lake Waramaug, a fine old inn with lovely rooms and excellent cuisine. The inn's beach across the road is for swimming and boating, and behind the inn is Pinnacle Mountain, with hiking trails and gorgeous views.

There is an embarrassment of riches at Lake Waramaug, not only the Boulders, but three more inns around the lake which rate four stars or four forks, or whatever means the best.

The next place you come to is the Hopkins Inn, but first we'll go the Hopkins Winery, just up the road from the inn. The winery is a pleasant place to visit. The people who run it are obliging and will take you on a tour of the vineyards and take you through the whole wine-making process until you raise your glass. You may sample the wines the Hopkins people make, red, white, and blush.

Across the road from the winery is the Hopkins Inn, a hostelry since 1945. It has its own beach and, when the weather is agreeable, you may dine on a wide, tree-shaded terrace. You

LAKE WARAMAUG

HOPKINS INN, NEW PRESTON

dine sumptuously at the Hopkins Inn. The telephone is (203) 868-7295.

The Inn on Lake Waramaug is down the road a mile or so. On the left is a broad lawn with boats beached or tied up and several sight-seeing craft. The Inn is up a gentle slope from the lake, large white, and beautiful. It's been an inn since the 1880s, a highly successful, top-grade place with, as you can imagine, a cuisine that is the best. There are big, pleasant rooms with fireplaces and bathrooms, and a wealth of activities all year round. The telephone is (203) 868-0563.

Keep going round the lake and near its head is a road that will take you to a private golf club. Go past the entrance and when you come to a T, turn right and before long on your left is a sign that says, "Constitution Oak Farm." It's a bed and breakfast, presided over by Mrs. Devaux. A kind lady, she will see to your every want. The farm is on a quiet road, old-fashioned and comfortable with huge trees around it. The telephone is (203) 354-6495.

Now please go back to the lake because we haven't finished there yet. Nearby is the Lake Waramaug State Park with a beach for boating and swimming and 88 campsites scattered throughout a wide area. It is clean and well-run with friendly people to answer your questions. The campground number is (203) 868-0220, and the park office is (203) 868-2592.

Keep going and soon you will come to the last of the inns on Lake Waramaug, The Birches, run by Heinz and Christa Holl. They are innkeepers in the finest European tradition. Heinz has long experience running inns here and abroad. The rooms are large and comfortable with lovely views over the lake. The inn has facilities for weddings and receptions, that sort of thing. The telephone is (203) 868-0229.

If you proceed around the rest of the lake you will go back to New Preston and be on your way up Route 202 to Bantam and Litchfield.

HAYING AT HOPKINS VINEYARD, NEW PRESTON

LITCHFIELD COUNTY WINE COUNTRY

If you would like to get lost in a wild and beautiful place for a spell, call Janet Gordon at (203) 927-3123. Take Route 45 to Warren and left on Route 341 until you get to Davis Road. Go right and soon left on Kenmont Road, which is dirt. After several miles you will pass through the buildings of a camp, and hanging on a tree is a sign that says, "Bromica Lodge 1 1/2 miles." Mrs. Gordon has a play area on the edge of the lake which, by the way, is North Spectacle Lake. It is spring-fed and clear. You may fish there. One more stop and we're on our way to Bantam. Take Route 341 to Warren, and pause for a moment. The little town of Warren was named for Revolutionary War General Joseph Warren, who was killed at Bunker Hill. The town is watched over by its beautiful Congregational church on the hill. It's worth a picture.

Continue on Route 341, and when it joins Route 202, go left and soon you will be at the entrance to Mount Tom State Park, on your right.

Head in and stick around. This is a neat place. In the park is Mount Tom, an easy way up so you may want to climb it. At the top is a stone tower. Beside the little park is a pond with all the amenities for having a good time, boating, swimming, changing, picnicking, food. You could kill half a day here very easily.

We're aimed at Bantam, but by the long way because the drive around Bantam Lake is so pretty. When you can tear yourself away from the park, proceed up Route 202 to Bantam, and when you get to Route 209, turn right. Down the road a little way is Cinema IV, a popular movie theater, whose number is (203) 567-0006. When you get to Route 109, turn left and left again onto Route 61, which will put you on Route 63 right beside the White Memorial Foundation, on your left. Scout around and find your way to the office.

The vision of a brother and sister, Alain C. White and May W. White, has given Litchfield County one of its prized gems, the beautiful tract you are about to prowl around in. The foundation and its 4,000 acres is devoted to conserving the environment, educating the public about its responsibilities, providing extensive recreational facilities, and establishing a center for study and research.

The White Memorial is on Route 202 and it almost sur-

CHURCH AT WARREN

rounds Bantam Lake. On the property are 35 miles of trails for hikers, horseback riders, snowshoers, and cross-country skiers. Canoeing is big on the lake. The White is also big on wildlife.

Near the entrance to the foundation is the White's handsome old house and a fine museum with mounted birds and animals, reptiles, insects, dioramas of what things looked like in the time of the glaciers and what they are like now. Upstairs is a large nature library and rooms for study and research.

All over this vast place are campsites and facilities for housing and feeding groups of students and others. There are field trips, lectures, nature study courses and programs for children. The White is quite a place. The telephone is (203) 567-0857. It draws people from all over, but it's big enough to absorb them all. From the windows there are lovely views of Bantam Lake.

Now, on to ancient, historic, beautiful Litchfield, the seat of this fascinating county. It was bought from the Indians for 15 pounds and named for the English cathedral city of Lichfield.

Litchfield's early opulence was due in part to Julius Deming, a wealthy merchant, who lived on North Street in the most pretentious house in town. Litchfield looks as if it had been restored like Williamsburg, but it hasn't. Many of its handsome old houses are just as they were when they were built two centuries ago. Some are still lived in by the descendants of their first owners.

You will be approaching Litchfield up Route 202 from Bantam, and in a moment you will be at the west end of one of the loveliest greens for miles around. It is long and wide and has streets on both sides. The right side is all stores and small businesses, with several restaurants.

We suggest a stroll so you can see for yourselves what a pretty town Litchfield is and savor what it has to offer. The other side of the green is old colonial houses, office buildings and the county jail that's been there since George Washington was in short pants. Back on the right side is the ancient county

CONGREGATIONAL CHURCH, LITCHFIELD

COUNTY COURT HOUSE, LITCHFIELD

courthouse and across the street ahead of you is a real prize, the
Litchfield County Historical Society and Museum.

Go, by all means. You won't want to leave until you have
been in every room. There are portraits of the Revolutionary
War era, old guns and statues, historic photographs, stained
glass, pottery, a good collection of pewter made by five genera-

MILTON EPISCOPAL CHURCH, LITCHFIELD

tions of the Danforth family, store signs from long ago, silver
and china and miniatures, ancient ball gowns, ancient dresses,
old-fashioned jewelry, examples of needlepoint.

North Street is across the green from the museum. It's wide, lined with huge trees, sidewalks, and lovely old mansions set in wide lawns. One of them, Sheldon's Tavern number 73, is where General Washington slept. On the left as you go away from town is a red house, smaller that its neighbors, always flying the American flag to mark it as the home of the Rev. Lyman Beecher, a notable divine and the father of even more notable children, Harriet Beecher Stowe, the author of *Uncle Tom's Cabin*, and Henry Ward Beecher, also a minister. Here we digress to give you this century-old ditty:

> There once was a preacher named Beecher
> Who said, "The hen is a wonderful creature!"
> The hen, just for that, laid an egg in his hat
> And thus did the hen reward Beecher.

Behind the shops on South Street is Cobble Court. Poke around until you find it. A fine book shop presided over by Anne Talcott, The Litchfield Exchange, and a kitchen shop with china pots and copper molds are among the things you will find here.

Down South Street, across the green on the right, is the country's first law school, founded by Tapping Reeve, whose wife was Aaron Burr's sister. The house is where Reeve held his first classes until there were too many students and he had to build a little one-room house next door. The big house is a beautiful, colonial treasure with stenciled wallpaper, portraits, and antique furniture. The paneling inside is stunning, the color of smoky honey. The school's graduates included men of distinction, legislators, two vice-presidents, and others, whose pictures you will see when you visit the little house next door. If you have a feeling for history, you'll love this place.

The big Oliver Wolcott Library is down the street on the same side. Back at the head of the green is the striking white Congregational church, one of the most photographed churches in New England. Down Route 118 a mile or so on the left is

HARRIET BEECHER STOWE

HENRY WARD BEECHER

Lourdes of Litchfield, a big spread of green lawns, statues, and a facsimile of the grotto at Lourdes in France.

The next left after Lourdes is East Litchfield Road. It will take you to Lee's Riding Stable, a year-round operation where there is an indoor ring, pony rides, and trail lessons. The number is (203) 567-0785. Across the road is the famous Haight Vineyard, a pleasant place with vines all around you. You will be treated to a tour and wine-tasting when you go there.

Some miles down Route 63 is the widely-known White Flower Farm, a big nursery with a huge reputation and an enormous variety of plants. The number is (203) 567-8789.

There are at least seven antique dealers in Litchfield and almost as many in Bantam. Among the stores on Route 202 as you go towards Bantam are a Mexican restaurant, LaTienda Cafe, (203) 567-8778; and Ming's, a Chinese restaurant, (203) 567-0809.

Beyond these two places, on the other side of Route 202, is the Litchfield Inn, a large inn for all seasons and all occasions, comfortable, its reputation well-earned, a place where you can have a cozy dinner for two by candlelight or a whopping big banquet. The telephone is (203) 567-4503.

On the other side of Litchfield, on the way to Torrington on the left, is the Litchfield Hills Nursery, a busy place that seems to have everything you could possibly need for your garden. Its number is (203) 567-9374. Beyond it, also on the left, is the Tollgate Hill Inn, so old and renowned that it is on the National Register of Historic Places. It's a popular place and rightly so because the food it serves is delicious. The number is (203) 567-4545.

Now let's go back to the green to wrap up this tour. Half way down Main Street is the Litchfield Food Company with all kinds of plain and exotic things and a deli. We suggest ordering sandwiches of your own devising, taking them out to the nearest

COBBLE COURT, LITCHFIELD

bench and devouring them while you look around at this wonderful New England town.

We'll see you on the fourth tour.

MARY FLOYD TALMADGE & HER CHILDREN, LITCHFIELD HISTORICAL SOCIETY

HILLSIDE BEAUTY

FOURTH TOUR

The fourth tour of exploration begins in the Litchfield Hills in the pretty little town of Bridgewater in the southwest corner of the county. Then it goes to Roxbury and on to Washington and Washington Depot.

BRIDGEWATER WAS PART OF NEW MILFORD UNTIL IT WAS set off as a separate town in 1856. Like many early churches, Bridgewater's was Congregational and, like so many early churches, it was cold. The parishioners had to suffer through two-hour sermons on Sunday. The women had it made, after a fashion. They had little foot stoves to warm their feet, but the men didn't. All they could do was knock their feet together to keep them alive.

Bridgewater is a village to savor, so drive slowly through its main street, and when you get to the Historical Society, stop! You will notice on your travels through Litchfield County that many of the little towns have historical societies and museums, archives where townspeople, prideful of their history, have brought their treasures to be preserved for the benefit of visitors and for coming generations.

All are run by volunteers, generally amiable ladies, who will open the door for you, take your modest fee, if there is one, and give you a tour. Most are closed in the winter, but if, like your explorer on his research, you have good reason to go, you can generally find somebody who will let you in.

The Bridgewater Historical Society is not just glass display cases and shelves with the town's treasures on them. When you go, you will be turning your clock back a century and stepping into the house of a vigorous and well-to-do family, the rooms furnished with all the things that made their lives work.

In the big living room is a spinning wheel, a gramophone with its horn, a horsehair sofa, pictures in Victorian frames of men in stiff collars and droopy moustaches, and their women in pompadour and lace, a big reed organ, an iron stove in front of the blocked off fireplace, the parlor table with the family photograph album and a stereopticon.

In the dining room are cupboards with the best china and glassware. The kitchen is large and dominated by the huge range with a pile of wood and a scuttle of coal beside it. The cream separator is on a shelf, and in one corner is an ancient clothes washing machine, probably the first edition of such a contrivance. In the pantry are cookie cutters, a rolling pin, and jars for canning everything under the sun.

There's a hobby horse in the playroom upstairs, and a doll house and a trunk overflowing with toys. Next door is the school room with little desks, the teacher's desk and old, old school books.

We hope you go to this fascinating old house with its powder horns, trophies, medals and old shoes, and — well, go and look.

Also on Main Street is a handsome Federal-Greek revival mansion, now an attractive bed and breakfast called the Sanford Pond House, run by its owners, George and Charlotte Pond. The rooms are large, uniquely decorated, with sitting areas and private baths. No children or pets, they say. The telephone is (203)355-4677.

Now rush on to Roxbury, not very far away. By the way, the Roxbury Fair is at the end of July.

VALLEY IN THE LITCHFIELD HILLS

If you like exploring, picnicking in pleasant spots, and hiking, these places will be hog heaven.

The first is the Mine Hill Preserve, a monument to man's aspiration and failure. In the middle of the 18th century, the scent of silver sent pick and shovel to scratch in the hills. No silver. Many years later the possibility of iron ore in them thar

FURNACE IN THE MINE HILL PRESERVE,
ROXBURY

hills sent the picks and shovels back again. This time, success blossomed.

Tunnels were dug, furnaces built with a little railroad to haul out the ore, a blacksmith shop, sheds, living quarters for the miners. The place hummed. Work went on until the price of steel dropped in the panic of 1873. Big mines in Minnesota and Pittsburgh dwarfed the little operation in Roxbury and put it out of business forever.

To get to the Mine Hill Preserve, leave Roxbury on Route 67, go over a new bridge and immediately turn right on Mine Hill Road. Follow the signs to Mine Hill and park. A narrow path leads down into the woods, and soon you will come to an oval sign that explains the paths through the preserve. It's wild and exciting and remote, with enormous blocks of granite, little ponds, streams and deep woods. Soon through the trees you will see massive granite structures with signs that tell you that they were ovens to roast the iron ore, and a blast furnace where the roasted ore was smelted to form iron. Beyond these monstrous furnaces and ovens are granite foundations that no one knows anything about. They are a riddle. This trail is marked by blue blazes, and the other one that leads to the mine tunnels is yellow blazed.

The paths are rocky and hazardous so , unless you are fleet of foot, take a stick. The area is lovely with dramatic scenery and pleasant walking trails. It's a haven for foxes, deer, bobcats, and other wild things. It's also great for birders. If you like cruising over back roads, try the roads around Mine Hill.

Not far south of Mine Hill is the River Road Preserve. It lies along the Shepaug River and is ideal for hiking and birding. Rivers are always fun. To get to this preserve, go out to Route 67 and head south. Soon you will come to Weller's Bridge Road. Turn left and almost immediately right on River Road. The preserve is down a little way on your right. If you are big on botany and geology, you will find this place just your ticket. The Shepaug floods occasionally and does strange things to the flora.

Under a canopy of hardwoods, you will find skunk cabbage and ferns and other wetland species. The area, being a flood plain, is subject to dramatic ecological changes, and if all this excites you, take your camera and notebook.

The next stop on this little adventure is the Tierney Preserve, down the road and around the corner. Go down River Road, hang a left onto South Street and immediately right onto Squire Road. The preserve is on you right. The trail is a three-and-a-quarter mile loop that skirts Jack's Brook and goes to a rocky cascade and pool.

The trail goes around the perimeter of the preserve, and on the way you will come to giant boulders, pushed south by the last glacier as it rumbled along 10,000 years ago. It pushed the boulders ahead of it and dumped them off, sometimes in a line where it stopped. They are called "boulder trains." We thought you'd like to know.

The Lilly Preserve is not far, so while you are still in the mood for exploring, head east on Squire Road, cross Route 67 and continue east on Rucum Road. A mile north will take you to Good Hill Road and the Lilly Preserve on your right, where you will find a parking area.

There is a blue trail and a yellow trail in the Lilly Preserve, and we suggest you stick to them because it gets swampy in the wet season and if you stray from the trails you're apt to get your feet wet. The whole area is 139 acres of interestingly varied terrain.

When you have done the Lilly, head out towards Roxbury on Good Hill Road. A short way north on Route 67 is a general store where the kind proprietor will give you maps of all these areas. The maps are courtesy of the Roxbury Land Trust.

The Beardsley-Humphrey Preserve is north on Route 199, less that two miles from Roxbury. You'll know when you get

FLORA OF LITCHFIELD COUNTY

trillium

tansy

violet

fox

wild *ginger*

mullein

barn swallow

♂

5-¾" - 7-¾"

downy
woodpecker

♂

5-¾"

rose-breasted grosbeak

♂

7-¼"

♂

ruby-throated
hummingbird
3"

♂

black-&-white
warbler
4-½"

blackpoll
warbler
4-½"

♂

♂ ♀

tufted
titmouse

5-½"

♂

scarlet
tanager
6-¼"

♀

tree
sparrow
5-¾" - 6-½"

♂

palm
warbler

4-½"

there because there is a utility pole with a blue blaze on it. These two preserves occupy the same general area. The Beardsley is marked by blue blazes and will take you two and a half hours if you want to do the whole thing. The Humphrey is only an hour and a half and yellow-blazed. That trail skirts both banks of Moosehorn Brook and flows into a deep and quite impressive gorge in what's known as the Caroline Glen at the east end of the preserve. The gorge is in a grove of tall hemlocks. Once you've got beyond the roar of the cascades, you'll find the area quiet and peaceful, and rewarding after your walks.

Now that you have done all those preserves, head north on Route 199. Before you get into Washington, on your left is the American Indian Archeological Institute (AIAI), one of the richest experiences Washington has to offer. A sign on Curtis Road will direct you to it.

For a small museum, this one packs a mighty punch and you will be well rewarded by a visit. If you haven't scheduled enough time, you'll wish you had.

The place is unique with its attractive and beautifully run exhibit hall, longhouse, gift shop, classrooms, and research facility. It is a center for the discovery, preservation, and inter-pretations of the lifeways of the first peoples of the northeastern woodlands. The outreach of the AIAI is enormous with guided tours on Saturday mornings at 11:30, workshops for study, self-guided walks on habitat trails, films every weekend, and opportunity to study the ways of the Indians.

Membership will bring you a wealth of benefits: meetings, publications, lectures, 10% discount in the museum shop, films, courses, and craft workshops. You don't have to do all these things, but do go and stay long enough to drink in the world of the first Americans. The number is (203) 868-0518.

A public-spirited man named Frederick W. Gunn founded the Gunnery School that is on your left as you head into Washington. It is a well-known college preparatory school. The

BIRDS OF LITCHFIELD COUNTY

beautiful old Congregational church that was built in 1741 is on one side of the green and the other sides are Gunnery School buildings. The green is vintage New England with giant maples around it.

Across the street are two buildings with Mr. Gunn's name on them. The first one you see is the Historical Museum of the Gunn Memorial Library. Please plan your trip so you go there when it's open.

All the little museums on our tours have different hours, and they are often limited because they are manned by volunteers. Call first. The Gunn Museum's number is (203) 868-7756. The curator is a kind and knowledgeable lady named Mary Harwood.

The house was built in 1781. It suffered architectural changes and is now a typical late-18th-century house of central hall design. All the things you will see in the museum are from Washington, a tribute to the people of this lovely town who have preserved their relics of the past. Downstairs is antique furniture, books, pictures, the things that make you know that it was once a loved and lived-in home.

Upstairs is amazing. There are comely models in two of the rooms, a collection of dolls that would make any girl's eyes pop out, a whole case of thimbles in uncounted numbers. The case revolves so you can see the little things better.

There are four-poster beds, a spinning wheel, all the things that made a colonial house work. You will see autographs of George Washington, Thomas Jefferson, and others, landscapes, and portraits, a fine collection of silver, china, and pewter. If you like old things, you won't breeze through the little museum.

The Gunn Memorial Library is next door. It's worth a good visit too. The interior is beautiful, fit to house a handsome collection of books. The collection spans from colonial times to right now. It's an up-to-date library with lovely stained-glass windows and fine woodwork.

CONGREGATIONAL CHURCH, WASHINGTON

AUTUMN WOODS & FIELDS
from a photo by Judy Mead

Roundabout are lovely old colonial houses, a neighborhood that invites a tour on foot.

Down Route 47, a short way on the left, is the famous Mayflower Inn, under renovation until early 1992. The number to call for information is (203) 868-9466.

Washington comes in two parts, Washington and Washington Depot, and that is because there was once a railroad. Washington Depot is where all the shops are, bank, post office, garage, a large and fine book store, The Hickory Stick, well-stocked and with a good second-hand section. It will search for out-of-print books.

Back of the Hickory Stick is a plaza with shops and the Pantry, a restaurant with an interesting gift shop that relates to food. A popular catering service is part of the establishment. The owner is Michael Ackerman. The number is (203) 868-0258.

Up the street on Route 47 in a modest building is Jonathan's, a fine little restaurant owned by Vincent Pauroso. The building may be small but there's nothing small about the menu, which is extensive, with finger food for kids and prices that are not out of sight. The telephone is (203) 868-0509.

Still farther up Route 47 is Dobber's Den, a small, nice looking restaurant with a bar and a pool table. The number is (203) 868-2239.

Keep going up Route 47 to another treat on the right, at a place where the road widens. Park and cross Bee Brook on a narrow bridge and you are in the Hidden Valley Reservation, a large and incomparably lovely region with the river winding through it, precipitous hills on either side, all interlaced with riding and hiking trails with vistas over the valley to higher hills beyond.

Back of the handsome town hall in Washington Depot in its own building is the Washington Art Association, old, established, busy, a vital element in the community. Washington's sophistication is evident in the exhibitions that the association

LITCHFIELD HILLS FARM

ROAD THROUGH THE WOODS

mounts. It doesn't have to search far for resident artists to put on a first-class art show.

You can go there for pottery lessons, figure drawing, print-making, drawing from life. There is a sculpture studio, a place where you can go to draw and paint with an instructor or without one. There are classes for children, from mud pie to clay. There is a faculty of professional artists. Members of the association go on bus tours to museums and theatrical perform-ances. There are lectures, films, and social functions. Things are not dull in Washington.

Before we leave Washington Depot and head north to con-quer new worlds, there is a wild and appealing region we wouldn't want you to miss.

Take the road beside the drugstore across the street from The Hickory Stick and the next left. This is River Road on the Shepaug. Another left and over a bridge and you will be on the edge of a green plain. A sign will tell you that you are in the Steep Rock Reservation. It also says no motorcycles. For some miles you will be right beside the river. The road is not for over 10 miles an hour. It's a lovely drive, nice also for bikes and walking. In the autumn, after the leaves have turned, it's gor-geous.

A mile and a half later there is a road to the left that is barred. A sign says, "E. S. Pinney Trail one and one tenth miles." Also another Steep Rock sign. Park across the road, walk around the barrier and into the woods. Soon you are on the ancient railroad bed. To the left it goes back to Washington Depot, so go to the right. The black hole in front of you is the tunnel that the trains years ago chugged through on their way north. It's apt to be cool and damp there. The tunnel is not very long and there's daylight around a curve. A pleasant little diversion.

There's more to this little toot than just the tunnel. Go back to your car and push on through the woods. The road winds and goes up with a steep bank on your left. There's another Pinney sign with a picnic area.

Now back to civilization and, after a satisfying respite, take a look at your map and see how to get to Bristol.

FIFTH TOUR

The fifth tour starts in Bristol, in the far southeast corner.
After going through Terryville, Plymouth, Thomaston,
Watertown, and Woodbury, it goes north to
Bethlehem and Morris.

THIS TOUR IS RICH IN PLACES TO GO AND THINGS TO SEE and it starts in Bristol down Route 6. This is as far east as we'll go.

When you get to King Street, turn right. Cross Route 72 and go on. Now you are on Lake Avenue and at its end is the biggest thing in the whole of Bristol, Lake Compounce Festival Park, which says it's the oldest such still running in the country. It's a happy, attractive place with things going round and round, up and down, rides, waterslides, paddle boats, an outdoor theater all summer. The number is (203) 583-6000.

When you have seen it all, head back into town. Go left on Route 6 and soon right on Route 69. Up the road a piece on the right is the Barnes Nature Center, a place with enough going on for you to spend a bit of time at. It's a museum with some displays that are alive and some that are not alive, a do-it-yourself trail system where you will wind your way through unusual habitats.

Before you leave Bristol, take a ride over to Route 72 to a big old brick building with an imposing front. It is the New

CAROUSEL MUSEUM, BRISTOL

England Carousel Museum. Go in and step back into your childhood. Bill Finkenstein, a jovial man, creates and restores merry-go-round horses, and you can tell by the look on his face that he loves his work.

The place is enormous, and as you walk down the aisle between the animals, they look at you with their big glassy eyes. This is a fun place to visit and the pleasant and happy atmosphere will wash over on you when you talk to Bill and his helpers. There are probably more wooden horses here than any place on earth. The oldest of Bill's beasts is a drop-out from Lake Compounce. No wonder. He first saw the light of day in 1870!

Bristol holds one more fascination for you: the American Clock and Watch Museum at 100 maple Street. Maple Street is Route 6 and there's an enormous clock on the front lawn.

Rarely in the history of mankind have so many people let their imaginations soar into such wild fancy to produce so much beauty, wit and kookiness as clockmakers.

The museum is in a large and handsome old colonial house whose rooms are ideal for a collection of way over 3,000 clocks and watches. It's an extraordinary institution, probably the only one of its kind in the world. It's a light-hearted place, alive down to the last tick. Will the drip of a water clock beguile you, or a mouse running up the Hickory Dickory Dock clock? The place is alive with clocks. A man takes all day, once a week, to wind up his charges.

Joyce Stoffers, the managing director, charming and very helpful, will answer your questions, unless she is busy answering somebody else's questions. The museum draws crowds.

Try to get there at noon. Eleven o'clock will do nearly as well. The grandfather clocks live in one big room with a high ceiling. A good thing, because one of them is a monster 13 feet high. The clocks all stand around talking together. You have to be in there with them at noon to believe the racket they make.

CLOCK & WATCH MUSEUM, BRISTOL

LITCHFIELD CLOCKFACE, ca. 1815

Boy! Is this place ever worth a visit! If you call — the number is (203) 583-6070 — who knows who or what will answer you.

Thomas F. Hennessey blew a spark into flame that became the Lock Museum of America. It is at 130 Main Street (that's

Route 6) in Terryville. He persuaded the state to donate the land for one dollar and raised enough on his own to put up his fine little building. It is now substantially endowed and is probably Terryville's brightest jewel.

Mr. Hennessey accumulated an amazing collection of every imaginable lock. His locks are in seven display rooms. Case after case with tiny padlocks and padlocks that look big enough to lock up the Q.E. 2. There are locks for safes, locks for jails, locks for milady's treasure chest. A mock-up with a button to push makes a hand come out; push the key in a lock with the mechanism cut away and turn it so you can see how the thing works.

In the Yale Room is the model of the mortise cylinder pin tumbler lock designed by Linus Yale, Jr., considered to be the greatest invention in the history of lock-making. It is, however, not without historical precedent. Nearby is a pin tumbler lock made in Egypt 4,000 years ago.

There are two floors of locks, and we venture to say that even if you don't give a hoot about locks, you will after you have visited this intriguing place. Call before you go to be sure it's open. The number is (203) 589-6359.

Plymouth is the next town west of Terryville on Route 6, and although there's little here to beguile visitors, a few miles south is Buttermilk Falls, a creamy white cascade, well-named, a place for cameras. The falls are in a scenic little preserve that can be hiked in 15 minutes.

You have to backtrack to Terryville to find the road in. Opposite the Lock Museum is South Eagle Street. Take it, then South Main Street. Go left, then right to Lane Hill Road, and there you are.

Come along now to Thomaston on Route 6 where Seth Thomas, the famous clockmaker, once had his factory. It's long gone but the influence of the architecture of his time is still all over Main Street,

LOCK MUSEUM, TERRYVILLE

Dominating the street is the famous old opera house, once the heart-beat of Thomaston's cultural life. It's a tall, stately gem, its window frames of white dressed marble.

Beside it is the equally handsome town hall and fire house. In that complex you are sure to find someone not too busy to take you upstairs and show you the theater, still well preserved

FIRE HOUSE THOMASTON

with ornate plastered frescoes, unusual ironwork in the seats and balcony, all harking back to a bygone era. The great old house is being slowly and carefully restored against the day when it will be back in its former glory.

The opera house was built on the site of the town's first cemetery over a century ago. Naturally, the graves and headstones had to be moved. And of course, things began to happen. Somebody called Ralph has been seen in the clock tower. People have heard the organ play all by itself. Sometimes the house lights go on and off even when there is no power. The opera house is worth a visit.

The big Thomaston dam on the Naugatuck River is a sight. Go up Route 8 and right on Route 222 to get there.

Now please go back to Route 8, and a short way south, go right on Route 6. Soon you will be at the entrance to the Black Rock State Park, "black" because the early settlers mined graphite here. It is one of the loveliest state parks you will see for miles around. The surroundings are very pretty, with a pond for swimming and a stream for fishing and 90 campsites. There is a wide area for field sports, trails for hiking and cross-country skiing, depending on your mood and the season. It's a well-run place with nature programs. We recommend it.

Watertown is the next stop on your trip south on Route 6. There's not much to see in this busy little town but the well-known Taft School and a golf club called Crestbrook where the public may have seasonal memberships. It is on Northfield Road, which is off Route 63 to the right. It has a restaurant, but we suggest you call if the season is waning. The number is (203) 274-5411. The club is open until the first heavy snow.

In the center of town there is a museum in a handsome old red brick Victorian mansion with a wide variety of treasures gathered from Watertown attics. There are photographs of an unsavory tramp called the leatherman who bummed his way from town to town clad in leather, a get-up of his own devising. People threw him bones out of the kitchen door.

It's a good little museum with a great doll collection, last century kitchen things and tools, Indian arrow and spearheads, doll buggies, little old school desks and a comely teacher with an apple in her hand.

The museum is at the junction of Route 63 near the Civil

OLD OPERA HOUSE, THOMASTON

Way monument. Next to the movie theater is the Hemingway Restaurant, whose number is (203) 274-5543. Across the street from Taft School are vintage Victorian houses.

Now to Woodbury, the oldest by decades of all towns in Litchfield County. It was settled in 1674 and originally comprised most of the surrounding towns.

In that faraway time, "the whole country now known as Litchfield County, together with the northern part of Fairfield and the western part of Hartford counties, presented uninhabited wilderness. The birds built their nests in its forests without being disturbed by the smoke of a single wigwam, and the wild beasts who made it their home, were startled by no fires save those of a transient war party or a wandering hunter." So said John W. DeForest in 1850 in his *History of the Indians of Connecticut.*

Then came the white settlers, dawn to dark hard-working people whose enterprise, labor, and imagination soon produced log cabins, houses with shingle roofs, churches, town halls, and communities. The great stone chimney with its flanking fireplaces was the heart of the house. Sometimes it had 20 flues. By the light of the fireplace the farmer could fashion his tools, wooden teeth for the rake and flail, spiles for tapping sugar maples, and make snowshoes. During the Revolution, people melted down their pewter plates and trenchers and made bullets by the bushel for Washington's army.

They broke and hetcheled the flax, made barrels, butter firkins, wash tubs, water buckets. They burned limestone and hauled it by ox cart to Hartford and Albany to exchange for household necessities, three days to Hartford and return. The wife worked on food and clothes, she made cloth from flax, bread from corn, sugar from maple sap. Meat was home-grown, home-cured. She made candles and soap, she got up early and stayed up late, industrious and thrifty. She bore huge families. No wonder she died young.

OLD HOUSE, WOODBURY

Neighbors helped one another clear fields of rocks and stumps. They made heavy peg-toothed harrows, dragged brush to scratch in the seed. A child carried a bag of corn, planting the traditional five kernels and chanted:

One for the bug
One for the crow
One to rot
And two to grow.

The common bread was "rye and injun" made of rye meal and corn meal mixed. The farmer's fields yielded rye, buckwheat, and corn. The gardens yielded beans, peas, turnips, parsnips, carrots, pumpkins, and squash. The families had deer meat, pork, turkey, goose, pigeons. Blossoming flax was blue as the heavens.

It took 20 tedious operations before flax was ready for spinning. Children old enough to walk were old enough to work. The children's song "Pop Goes the Weasel" was to lighten one childhood chore, winding yarn onto a flaxwheel. One hundred turns and a small button known as a weasel would pop out, telling the child to stop turning.

Seed was imported from England because native grass was inferior. Irrigation ditches were used to improve the soil. Carrots were fed to cows to impart yellow to the butter.

Farmers and their families made all their own tools, rakes, hay forks, axe helves, shovels with wrought iron edges, flails, baskets, ox yokes, cheese presses, plows, all from the wood and iron at the door.

Starting in the 17th century, little factories sprang up. Saw mills, paper mills, grist mills turned the region into an industrial beehive. Busy Yankees made shears and thimbles, things out of silver, brooms and boxes for matches, hats, tile and pottery, cords for pendulums, rope and twine, wooden things, wheels

GLEBE HOUSE, WOODBURY

and tool handles. They made cigars and suspenders, carpet tacks and spectacles.

You will see the flowering of the settlers' inventiveness and industry as you go on this fifth tour because Woodbury, with its ancient houses and two museums, has preserved so much of its past.

Go slowly through the main street, not only because you will see more, but also because the traffic is often something to contend with. On your left as you go up Main Street is the Curtis House, a lovely old inn that has been where it is since 1745, the oldest inn in Connecticut. It advertises, "Every modern comfort, every ancient charm."

Two places on this tour are on our must list, the Glebe House and the Hurd House. Both are on Hollow Road, which goes to the left off Main Street. A glebe is a minister's homestead, his house and his grounds. The Glebe House in Woodbury is probably the most celebrated in New England because of its fine state of preservation, but equally important because it was in this house, only weeks after the end of the Revolutionary War, that the Rev. Dr. Samuel Seabury was elected bishop, the first in the new world. He went to England to be consecrated, but the stuffy Church of England wouldn't do it, so the good man had to go to Scotland instead.

The Glebe House is an ancient beauty, architecturally and historically. After its restoration in 1925 it became one of the early house museums with its old smoky honey woodwork, its priceless old furniture, its creaky stairs, its huge collection of treasures. The gardens are restored to their early state.

It is on the National Register of Historic Places, and fulfills itself in usefulness. It is more than a gorgeous old house to visit. It mounts activities for children and grown-ups, like learning to cook with 18th-century utensils, and learning to play 18th century games. It arranges historical tours and archeological digs, and brings history alive for people of all ages. To find out what goes on, call (203) 263-2855.

Two doors down the street is a little treasure, the Hurd House. John Hurd was Woodbury's first miller. The house has gone through several restorations, the oldest part dating from 1680. The different floor levels reflect the fact that two little houses were once put together. Every piece of furniture, every

HURD HOUSE, WOODBURY

CURTIS HOUSE, WOODBURY

candlestick, all the other relics you will see are museum pieces beyond price. The man to call to get in is a kind and friendly docent named Fred Strong. His number is (203) 263-3169.

Woodbury is the antiques capital of Litchfield County, and when you browse among the dozens of shops you'll think Woodbury is the antiques capital of America. Maybe it is.

We can't possibly mention all the antique dealers in Wood-bury because there are more than 35, so we'll confine ourselves to the largest, Mill House. It's huge. The main building was a 17th-century grist mill. It and seven other buildings are all stuffed with antiques, superior things like Heppelwhite, Shera-ton, and Chippendale. The place is prideful of its wares. It is several miles north of Woodbury, on Route 6. The telephone is (203) 263-3446.

Something else adds to Woodbury's lustre, the Woodbury Ski and Racquet Area, an all-year operation owned by Rod Taylor. It welcomes the public in winter for its cross-country and downhill skiing, lit at night on man-made snow when the real stuff isn't there. It has 200 km of cross-country trails.

The area has been there for 20 years. It has a lodge, a ski shop, lessons, and rentals. It is four and a half miles north of Wood-bury on route 47. The telephone is (203) 263-2203. It has two half-pipes for skateboarding and snowboarding. In summer it has music festivals specializing in reggae which, if you don't know, is Jamaican and African music.

At the junction of Route 6 and Route 64 is the Olive Tree Restaurant, whose number is (203) 263-4555, and at 146 South Pomperaug Avenue is the Milestone Motel. Its number is (203)263-2800. The owner is Marjorie Cassidy.

We have a treat for you now, the Flanders Nature Center, whose holdings are in several locations north and south of the town of Woodbury. Under the protection of the center are over 2,000 acres of wetlands, ponds, marshes, streams, woodlands, fields, and wonderful walks.

First you should go to the main office on Flanders Road, which branches to the left off Route 6 several miles north of Woodbury. There you can get filled in on what goes on in this big, lovely part of the world, tours, nature classes, films, lectures, wildflower and fern walks, bird walks and, in season, ample sugar gatherings. The telephone is (203) 263-3711.

FLANDERS WILDLIFE CENTER

South of Woodbury on Route 64 is the Whittemore Sanctuary, 700 acres of forests and woodlands, cross-country and hiking trails, and a pond.

At the nearby VanVleck Farm Sanctuary you can learn compass skills and map reading, and how not to get lost. Much of what goes on there is for children, adults too, of course.

This whole big nature center is waiting for you to explore. If you like the big outdoors, birds, animals, and flora, this place is for you.

Where we take you next is the little town of Bethlehem, which, as you can imagine, is a big splash at Christmas time, reverent wide-eyed children, madrigal singers and sight-seeing on a horse-drawn hayride. The town is lit up and decorated. The post office is deluged because everyone wants his Christmas cards mailed in Bethlehem.

The Christmas Shop on Route 61 is a beguiling place with every imaginable thing relating to Christmas, Easter too. Go and see for yourself its enormous array of toys and ornaments, gnomes, and Santas, delicately crafted models of wise men and Charles Dickens houses. It's a wonderful place for gifts and collectibles. The Christmas Shop is big at Easter and huge at Christmas. The telephone is (203) 266-7048.

Another of Bethlehem's prizes is the biggest creche you ever saw. There is only one other in the world. It is on Route 61 on the grounds of the Abbey of Regina Laudis, housed in its own building. It is enormous, a famous 18th-century Neopolitan Creation.

Fifty feet south of Flanders Road and Route 61 is a nursery you shouldn't miss. It is the Bethlehem Nursery, owned by Dennis Dodge, a grower and propagator of rare, drawf conifers. Mr. Dodge will welcome people who would like to wander around in his nursery. His number is (203) 755-1487.

There is one more thing we would like you to see in Bethlehem, the Wood Creek Cooking School. It is not just any old

LITCHFIELD HOUNDS, HUNT CLUB, BETHLEHEM

OLD TOWN HALL MUSEUM &
ONE ROOM SCHOOL HOUSE, MORRIS

cooking school. It was created by Terry Frank, internationally renowned for his "Get Cooking Connecticut" TV show, and his partner, Charlotte Libov. The classes at Wood Creek are small, intimate, and fun. Frank is a food expert who cooks, teaches, and writes about the culinary arts. There's not a country on earth whose menus he is not familiar with.

VALLEY IN MORRIS

To get to the school, take Route 47, which branches to the left a short way north of Woodbury. Soon, branch to the right on Route 132. Several miles later, Route 132 turns right. Go straight on Carmel Hill Road, turn right on Arch Bridge Road, and left on Judson Lane. The school is on your left. The telephone is (203) 266-5904.

LAKE AT MORRIS

With Vaughn Gray's map you shouldn't have trouble finding your way back to Bethlehem, so take Route 61 to Morris, the last stop on this tour.

Morris was named for Revolutionary War hero and famed educator James Morris, who founded and ran the Morris Academy for not quite a century. Morris looks just like the crossroads of Route 61 and Route 109. It isn't. It's a neat little town. At the corner are two small colonial buildings, the Morris Historical Society, built in 1861, and the Mill School, dated 1772. Both are museums housing the treasures of Morris' past, gathered and lovingly cared for by devoted townspeople. You will see the sleigh which a doctor of long ago used in his house calls, meticulously preserved and bright, shiny red, a collection of commemorative bottles, showcases from a country store filled with ancient merchandise, farm tools, antique dolls and cradles, arrowheads, buttons still sewn on cards, homely things dear to the people of the early days.

There is more to Morris. Down Route 109 to the east and through East Morris is a road that will take you on a long and lovely drive through the woods that skirts several reservoirs with a high dam and a waterfall.

Back through the crossroads at Morris and west on Route 109 will take you to Camp Columbia, a camp of 600 acres, long abandoned by Columbia University, now a place for pleasant walks to the edge of the White Memorial Foundation and Bantam Lake.

And here we shall leave you to get cranked up for the sixth and last tour on this Litchfield Hills adventure.

SIXTH TOUR

The sixth and last tour begins in Goshen. It goes to Torrington and Harwinton, then to Riverton, Winsted, Colebrook and ends in storied Norfolk.

WE LEFT YOU IN MORRIS, SO PLEASE HEAD NORTH ON ROUTE 63 through Litchfield, which we did on the fourth tour, to Goshen. On your way you will pass the Goshen fairgrounds where big, noisy things go on, especially over the Labor Day weekend.

The Connecticut Agricultural Fair is held the last week in July, the 4H Club in August, the Scottish Games in October after the big Goshen fair. If you like country fairs, this one in Goshen is one of the best in Litchfield County.

When you get to the rotary in Goshen, turn left. If you like bashing around in your boat on a pretty little pond and catching fish or just like being on the water, look for a boat launch sign on the left and head in. The road will take you to Dog Pond. The stuff the state puts out says you can catch large mouth bass and yellow perch. Happy fishing!

We have two more boat launches to tell you about. Keep going a short way to a boat launch sign that will guide you to West Side Pond, which is about the same size as Dog Pond, and another sign that will take you to Tyler Lake, one of the prettiest around.

Like so many New England towns, Goshen is prideful of its heritage. In 1990 Goshen's Quadrimillenium Committee published a handsome history called *Goshen, Connecticut, A Town Above All Others*. "This is not," the book says, "indicative of a chauvinistic snobbery on the part of the people of Goshen, but because it is the highest in altitude of any township in the state," according to the *Connecticut Historical Collections*, said in 1836.

The heartbeat of Goshen is its Historical Society and Museum, housed in a beautiful white colonial building west of the rotary, with a big shiny gold eagle over the door. It is a treasure house of Goshen's past with two floors of antiques, nostalgic reminders of the things their ancestors left them, collected with loving care by people who love their town and cherish their old relics, old books and bottles, an ages-old collection of scrap books, which is kept current. In one corner are several ancient school desks and a blackboard. Today's children get a kick out of sitting at those desks and reading the school books their forbears used.

In another corner is a table set for the kind of meal that was served in the 18th century. The society's collections include old cheese presses and cheese boxes, tools used indoors and out. There are show cases with antique jewelry, china, sea shells and butterflies, portraits of Goshen people through the centuries with their wooded faces, an impressive collection of pewter, the fearsome instruments doctors used long ago, a melodeon, the toys kids played with back then, treasures that families with deep Goshen roots have donated to the museum.

There is a warm, pleasant atmosphere in the society's rooms when the ladies gather to work on their collections. There are other museums in other towns that are as lovingly cared for as the one in Goshen, but none that is its superior.

The hours are posted on the door, but we suggest you call before you go. The number is (203) 491-9610.

There is more to this little town we'd like you to see, so go

GOSHEN HISTORICAL SOCIETY

to the rotary and turn right on Route 4, then left into a little shopping center. It is dominated by Bob's Village Market, a good store run by friendly and courteous people, and by Rich's well-stocked hardware store. The Goshenette is there, a busy little restaurant run by Lynn Zeller that prides itself on serving the best food.

Next to it is Pat Steier's PS Gallery, larger than you would expect. Pat attracts the work of the best artists in this region and elsewhere. If you like to browse in galleries, this one you should not miss for its good collection of pictures, sculptures, and unique jewelry. The number is (203) 491-4175.

Marilyn Nardozzi's Touch of Elegance is nearby, where you will find gifts, specialties, and crafts.

We have several other places to whet your appetite before we leave Goshen. Go back to the rotary and turn right on route 63. Soon on your left is Nodine's Smoke House where you can get smoked hams, turkeys and other meats of the highest quality, jams and jellies, candies and condiments, and delicious cookies. The store's number is (203) 491-4009. Nodine's also has a large mail order business, whose number is (203) 489-3213.

Go on a bit farther and on your right is a sign on Heady Lane directing you down a long driveway to the Heady Lane Herb Gardens, a neat and well-kept establishment where you can get every kind of herb that has a name, and dried flowers prettily done up. The enterprising lady who runs the place, Cindy Barrett, gives lessons at various times of the year on making baskets and wreaths, herbal cooking, and how to dry flowers that hang in bunches from the ceiling. Outside is a greenhouse, and beyond it are extensive herb and flower gardens. The little store has a light-hearted atmosphere and we recommend a visit to browse and drink in the titillating aromas. Call for times when Cindy and her staff give cooking lessons. The telephone is (203) 491-HERB.

This wraps up our visit to Goshen and we head east on Route

HERB GARDENS, GOSHEN

4 to Torrington, one of the two cities in Litchfield County. The other is Winsted.

Torrington is a thriving little city that fulfills the needs of a wide area. One of its assets is its trails, miles and miles of trails for walking, cross-country skiing, enjoying nature in the home of chipmunks, wild turkeys, and deer through forests of spruce and hemlock, ferns and wildflowers and mountain laurel.

When you hit Main Street, turn left and go on until you pass the North End Fire Station on one side and a little church on the other. Turn left on Newfield Road and you will soon be in the big Paugnut State Forest, a spread of nearly 2,000 acres that stretches from Torrington to Winchester.

You will find blue blazes marking the John Muir Trail. John Muir, bearded like a prophet, was one of our great naturalists and founder of the Sierra Club. This wild and beautiful area is woodsy roads and trails, meat and drink for the explorer. At the northern end is Burr Pond State Park, a lovely little place, carefully maintained, a mecca for picnicking and swimming, fishing and boating, but don't go over five miles an hour. Keep going and soon you will come to Taylor Brook, a big and attractive campsite, which is at the foot of big Highland Lake.

Now back to Torrington because we have more exploring to do. On Main Street there is an old and renowned hotel, the Yankee Pedlar, which has been there for many years. The number is (203) 489-9226. On East Main Street are three good restaurants all in the same block, Dick's, Le Rochambeau, and the Venetian. There's not a dud among them.

On Main Street, up two blocks on the right, is the Hotchkiss-Fyler House, so splendid a building that it is on the National Register of Historic Places. The brochure says, "Men wore gold chains and watch fobs, ladies anchored Merry Widow hats with jeweled hatpins, little girls wheeled doll carriages, and little boys rolled black iron hoops when the Hotchkiss-Fyler House was built by Orasmus Roman Fyler."

HOTCHKISS TYLER HOUSE, TORRINGTON

HISTORICAL SOCIETY MUSEUM, TORRINGTON

The house is a treasure, spotlessly maintained with its gold-leaf stenciled wallpaper, delicate Meissen and Dresden china figurines, and elaborately carved woodwork. The main hall reflects the opulence of the mansion's 16 rooms and glows with the richness of mahogany paneling.

Go, by all means. Next door is a far older house, the Torrington History Museum, and its collection of artifacts that reflects Torrington's ancient origins when the town cradled the brass industry, made clocks, and ice skates, and roller skates, and woolen uniforms. It's a great little museum in a beautifully restored, centuries-old house with two floors of exhibits that change periodically to cover Torrington's growth from its primitive beginning.

By the way, John Brown, the great abolitionist, was born in Torrington, and President Taft was entertained at the Fyler mansion in 1906.

Down Route 4 a little way from Torrington is Harwinton, a town carved out of the wilderness by Hartford and Windsor. The people of Harwinton, who care for their home, have preserved much of its history.

A bit west of where Route 4 joins Route 118 is a one-room school house, very much as it was when the last class was dismissed many years ago. Under the hinged top of her desk the teacher wrote the names of her last pupils. Next to the school is a barn with an admirable collection of farm tools from the past.

Inside the door is the canvas truss that was used to hoist oxen off the floor so they could be shod. Clumsy creatures, oxen can't stand on three legs. You will see an old sleigh, a shiny red delivery wagon, a forge, plows, a wagon jack, a shingle mill, butter churns, a winnowing machine, an incubator for baby chicks, and dozens of tools.

The modern school is next door, and frequently the kids troop over to the little schoolhouse to learn how things were a long time ago, and then they go to the museum to learn what all those things were and how they worked.

If you would like to visit these two places, call Mrs. Thierry at (203)485-1202 or Mrs. Stephenson at (203)485-1423. These charming and amiable ladies will respond to you.

There are two restaurants in Harwinton and two general stores all on Route 118.

South of the town is a 2,000-acre tract, the gift of J. Henry Roraback. It is a wildlife preserve named in his honor for his fellow townsmen to use. On Buell Pond is the Allen M. Heflin Wildlife Sanctuary.

Another of the town's treasures is the Theodore A. Hungerford Memorial Library, a Greek building which is soon to be refurbished for a historic museum, the home of Harwinton's possessions: stuffed owls, swords and guns, ancient dresses, a melodeon, candle holders, china, pictures, rocks and medals, and things packed away in boxes awaiting the day when they will be on view.

Harwinton people are proud of their fair which has been held since 1853. It's the first weekend in October.

At the junction of Route 118 and Route 4 is a recreation area, a lovely spot with a playground and a pavilion for picnics, tennis courts, a pond for fishing and frogging, but no swimming.

And this is the rundown on Harwinton, a charming little town.

The next stop on our journey is New Hartford. You could go back to Torrington on Route 4, right on Route 202, left on Route 219, and run right into New Hartford. Shorter and more fun are the back roads. Beyond the library-museum is Harmony Hill. It's off Route 118 to the left. It will take you to Cotton Hill Road, which runs into Route 202. Go right on Route 202 and soon left on Route 219. On the left is a big sign that says, "Trinita." Take the next right, which is Hoppen Road and left on Steele Road to an attractive bed and breakfast on your left, called Cobble Hill Farm, a lovely old house, a warm, welcoming atmosphere, and well-furnished, comfortable rooms. The people who run it are Jo and Don McCurdy. Their number is (203) 379-0057.

Not far away on Route 44 is another bed and breakfast called the Alcove. The telephone is (203) 693-8577. One of its rooms accommodates a wheel chair. The house is two miles south of New Hartford.

Yet another bed and breakfast, small and tucked away, is the Rose and Thistle, run by Lorraine Longmoor. To get there take the Ski Sundown road on Route 219 and the second right on Lavender Road. This is a dirt road. Go to its end and there is the Rose and Thistle. The number is (203) 379-4744.

Steele Road will take you past Pine Meadow, a pleasant place for a picnic, and into New Hartford. It is a town with handsome last-century buildings. If you take all the cars off the streets, you will be back in 1880. The buildings have parapets and turrets and beautiful brickwork. The building which the library and the Historical Society are in has been there since 1818. In one of those historic buildings, the New Hartford House, Elias Howe, whose pictures show him with a determined eye, invented the sewing machine.

If you are a ski enthusiast, don't miss a visit to Ski Sundown. Go east out of New Hartford on Route 219, up the west shore of Lake McDonough to the Ski Sundown sign. This famous place is a first class operation, lifts, trails, and slopes for every level of skier, and night skiing as well. There is no lodging at Ski Sundown, but there is a ski school, shop, rentals, a cafeteria, and a bar.

Go back to Route 219 and north along Lake McDonough, which is dwarfed beside the huge Barkhamsted Reservoir. Lake McDonough is for swimming, boating and fishing. The area between the lake and the reservoir is lovely with hiking trails, walks along spillways and waterfalls. There is a trail going up the long bank to the immense dam. The telephones for information about this area are (203) 379-3036 and (203) 278-7850.

Route 219 going north meets Route 318 which winds up and over the dam. The Barkhamsted Reservoir is so long you can't see its end. Route 318 will take you to a bridge over the West Branch of the Farmington River. You are at the south end of

BARKHAMSTED RESERVOIR

4,000 acres of one of the county's most spectacular places. Two state forests join here, the American Legion State Forest on the west side of the river and the People's State Forest on the east.

Let's take the west side first. This is the American Legion State Forest, an area of 782 acres, named for its donor. The road runs along the river with pleasant sights, the headquarters of a colony of turkey vultures, parking places for picnics, a camping area and a little way up, a blue-blazed trail. It goes up through the forest to the ruins on an old cheese box mill, then climbs the popular Tremendous Cliffs where, as you might expect, the view is worth the effort.

Along the road are places where you can fish, hunt, and go camping and hiking. Riverton lies on the other side of the river, so please go back to the bridge and head up the east shore where good sights await you.

There are five trails, all marked: an orange, two yellows, a red, and a blue. The two yellows are in different parts of the forest, so you won't get them mixed up. We guarantee you a good time exploring this big patch of woods.

For any information you think might need, call the Department of Environmental Protection, Office of State Parks and Recreation at (203) 378-7321. Here you can do everything you did on the other side of the river, and you can use your snowmobile.

The roads on both sides of the river will take you to Riverton, a neat little town dominated by what Lambert Hitchcock created in 1818, a factory for making his finely crafted and now celebrated chairs. The factory is still there along the river. Hitchcock chairs, hand stenciled with century old techniques, are still being built. An extensive showroom of sturdy and stylish furniture is there for you to browse in.

There are two telephone numbers: for Connecticut residents, 236-1223, and all others, toll free 1-800-772-7018.

Across the way is a prize of an old New England inn, the Old

OLD RIVERTON INN

Riverton Inn, in service since 1796 as a coach stop and tavern, now run with care and good taste by Mark and Pauline Telford. The food and the service are above reproach and the rooms are pleasant and comfortable. There is a welcoming atmosphere about the old inn that is very appealing. "Hospitality," they say, "for the hungry, thirsty, and sleepy."

Down the road a little way is a yummy little lunch place called the Catnip Mouse Tearoom, which says its lunches are "deliciously different."

Riverton is not very big, so poke around its streets with their appealing shops for a look at old New England.

Now, on to Litchfield County's second city, Winsted, a short run down Route 20 from Riverton.

Winsted is a family town with good shops and good restaurants. Among them are Jessie's on Main Street. The telephone is (203) 379-0109. Across the river on Rowley Street is the Tributary, which is large on sea food and steaks. Its number is (203) 379-7679. Another is Consetto's, a family place that was in Winsted long before the flood of 1955. It seats over 100 and its menus are Italian, English, and other things. The telephone is (203) 379-6911. It's a short way west of the hospital.

There is an Italian restaurant owned and run by its chef, Mike Monaco. Mike's number is (203) 379-6648. It is just west of the big Catholic church. And a Mexican restaurant at 576 Main Street called Cafe de Olla seats 54 people and serves Cajun food as well as Mexican on a large menu. Its number is (203) 379-6552.

On the west side of the city and looking down on it is the Solomon Rockwell House, built in 1813, a columned, Greek revival mansion, locally known as Solomon's Temple. Mr. Rockwell made his pile in the iron industry. The handsome old house is the repository of a variety of memorabilia of last-century Winsted, guns and portraits, china, a hobby horse for a young rider of long ago, books and maps, a good arrowhead collection, clocks and furniture. To match the house, the privy has carved Ionic columns and dentils. It's an interesting place with a splendid view. The telephone is (203) 379-8433.

Across Route 4 from Jessie's and a block west of the college is an attractive bed and breakfast run by Paul and Helga Wooden. The Provincial House is family-oriented and open all year. The number is (203) 379-1631.

If boating interests you, there is a boat launch on West Hill Pond. Go east on Route 44, and after a big car dealership on the right and a shopping center on the left, look for West Hill Road. Go right, and right again on Perkins Road to the pond.

You'd think that tiny Winchester was part of much larger Winsted, but it's the other way around. Winchester is the township and Winsted is part of it. Winsted, by the way, gets its *win* from Winchester and its *sted* from Barkhamsted.

Go west on Route 44 from Winsted and left on Route 263. You will soon have a glimpse of Big Highland Lake on your left. There is a boat launch at the north end of the lake, and fishing should bring you trout, largemouth bass, kokanee, and yellow perch. Maybe others.

Route 263 will take you to the little, unspoiled, typically New England town of Winchester. Slow down when you get to the green. Old houses surround it. A more pleasing scene would be hard to find. The church is in front of you, and to its right is a handsome gray house with pillared porch. Its owner is George Sherwood, and if you find him at home and in the mood to give you a house tour, you will be lucky. Mr. Sherwood is Winchester's postmaster, historian, and creator of the Kerosene Lamp Museum, surely the only one of its kind in the world.

Oil lamps became obsolete when electricity came to Winchester in the 1930s. That's when George and his wife began their collection. Their museum shares half the building next to George's house with the post office. There are more than 500 lamps hanging from the ceiling, on tables, and on the floor. Their variety begs description. There are large and ornate brass lamps that are lowered on chains to be cleaned and filled, lanterns that went on cabooses, headlights from ancient motor

FISHING ON THE HOUSATONIC

KEROSENE LAMP MUSEUM

cars. Such an example of creativity you can't imagine unless you go to the little museum and see for yourselves.

Beside the lamp museum and the post office, a dirt road goes off into the woods. Long ago it was a stagecoach road that went to Norfolk.

At about the time the stagecoaches were rumbling through the woods, a snake pit of bitterness and controversy opened about the location of the new meeting house.

"Arguments were rubbed out in wash tubs, invectives strung on clothes lines, epithets were churned in with butter," until the brouhaha reached white heat. One faction was so disgusted with the whole sorry affair that they packed up the possessions they could stuff in their wagons and headed west for new pastures. They abandoned everything else, including their houses.

The unhappy people even took their minister, the Rev. Publius Virgilius Booge with them. Their way led through what is now Lake Winchester, which didn't exist then.

North of the lake is Silas Hall Pond. There are quicksands in Silas's pond and one day poor Silas vanished.

The unused road is kept only as a fire lane. Otherwise, it's all yours, explorers, to hike over, drive over, and use for cross-country skiing. A little poking around along the road will disclose cellar holes where houses once stood, a bit of rusty farm equipment, and huge lilac bushes.

All this happened in 1797. The new home of the poor, disgruntled people is Vernon Center, New York, which is near Utica.

The second to the last town on this Litchfield County tour is a little Colebrook, tucked away in the northeast corner of the county and reached by taking Route 263 to Route 44 where you turn left, and soon right on Route 183.

Settled in 1765, Colebrook is hilly and so densely covered with pines and hemlocks that it was called "The Green Woods." It looks today much as it must have then, and when you see this

gem of a village you are likely to say, "Let's keep this place secret!"

In the early 1800s there were nearly twice as many people in Colebrook as there are now, and that is because there were factories then that made chairs, paper, hats, cider, shingles, wagons, and no doubt other things.

A classic little building on the main street is the town hall and the historical society, presided over with devoted care by its curator, and if you want to know when the place is open, call (203) 379-3509.

The society's museum is one of the best, with a wide-ranging collection of Colebrook's treasures gathered by its citizens, aware of their home's history and anxious to preserve it. Its rooms are colorful with their displays: uniforms from all our wars, a big collection of flags, guns, swords, and powder horns, tools and pictures and silverware and china.

There is a lap organ that ministers used in their services long ago, a self-heating flatiron (you'll have to ask the lady in charge how it worked), a bed with glass casters which protected you from lightning if you were in it, a machine for shearing sheep, and, well, go and visit this enchanting little house and see for yourselves. Across the street is an historic landmark, the Colebrook General Store, in continuous use since 1811, a handsome building with a columned front. And down the street, rising from the dark background of conifers, is the gleaming white Congregational church, modeled after Charles Bullfinch's designs.

After you've drunk in the beauties of this lovely little town, head west on Routes 182 A and 182, which take you to Route 44 and into the colorful and historic town of Norfolk, last stop on this safari and a one-of-a-kind town.

Norfolk was late settling because it's rocky and hilly and the winds roar down from the north. It's known as the ice box of

MAIN STREET, COLEBROOK

1812 GENERAL STORE, COLEBROOK

Connecticut, cold in the winter but delightfully cool in the summer.

In 1860 when it was proposed that a railroad be built into Norfolk, someone said, "Build a railroad through Norfolk? Why even the crows have a hard time flying over those hills!" Farmers were not attracted to Norfolk, but rich people from far away were. They built their big estates and lived a gay social life in the bracing mountain air. Norfolk became to Connecticut what Lenox was to Massachusetts a century ago, in those halcyon days before the income tax siphoned off much of their wealth.

Before that dismal situation arose, two enormously wealthy families, the Battells and the Stoeckels, left their estates in a trust to be used by the Yale School of Music. The school was host to Sergei Rachmaninoff, Jean Sibelius, Alma Gluck, Ernestine Schumann-Heinck, Victor Herbert and other notable musicians. Besides a magnificent mansion, the donors had a music shed built that holds 1,200. The Yale School of Art is also big in Norfolk. For tickets and information during the summer, call (203)542-5537.

As you approach Norfolk from the east, the road curves around to the left, and at the curve, over your right shoulder, are two stone pillars marking the entrance to the Dennis Hill State Park. Drive in, and in a minute you will come to clipped fields on both sides of the drive. It's a quiet, peaceful area with picnic benches with pleasant views. You can drive or walk up to the top of the hill where there is a big sprawling stone pavilion, long unused and open to the winds. It was built years ago by Dr. Frederic Dennis for the pleasure of his guests. The views from the airy hilltop are stunning.

A short way beyond the entrance to this park is the old established Hillside Garden, owned and run by a distinguished couple, Mary Ann and Frederick McGourty, who years ago created an unusual and beautiful nursery. It is informal, with no laid-out beds. The broad and hilly lawns are drifts of color with perennials of every kind of flower that will grow there.

Both McGourtys are respected gardeners, writers, lecturers, and the authors of many books. It's a joy to stroll through their gardens, then visit the sales area, which is a garden-lover's and garden-shopper's paradise. The telephone is (203) 542-5345. Gardens and nursery are open from May 1 through September.

Norfolk is a cut apart from all the towns you have seen in your travels around Litchfield County. Its sophistication is apparent from the handsome buildings only wealth could have built. The lovely, homey Norfolk Library, the gift in 1889 of Isabella Eldridge, is a good example. The atmosphere is friendly and Miss Eldridge's portrait by Ellen Emmet Rand hangs where everyone can see it, and from where Miss Eldridge can look down on her creation. Miss Eldridge was at the library every morning while it was being built and long afterwards to watch over it. One morning she was sweeping the dead leaves off the front porch when a stranger approached and asked if there was a portrait of the founder. "Yes," Miss Eldridge replied. She led him in and pointed out the picture of herself. The man looked at it, then gave her a quarter saying, "My good woman, you are serving a good cause."

The library, its fine architecture, stained glass windows, everything about it was her devoted concern. It is a gathering place for the people of Norfolk, with pleasant reading rooms, concerts, and art shows.

The Norfolk Historical Society is in a classic little building on Main Street. It is a museum housing a splendid collection; on two floors Norfolk's relics are carefully preserved and displayed. Prominent among these things are the papers, books, maps and other memorabilia of those three Norfolk families, the Battells, Stoeckels, and Eldridges, whose wealth and influence are woven deeply into the fabric of their home.

In this splendid little museum you will find genealogical books, old costumes, railroad lanterns and other treasures.

Across the street is an unusual fountain, designed by famed architect Stanford White. It has three levels of watering troughs, the lower one for dogs, the middle one for horses, and the top one for people. In the Battell chapel of the Church of Christ, is a triumph of beauty, five magnificent Louis Comfort Tiffany

NORFOLK HISTORICAL SOCIETY

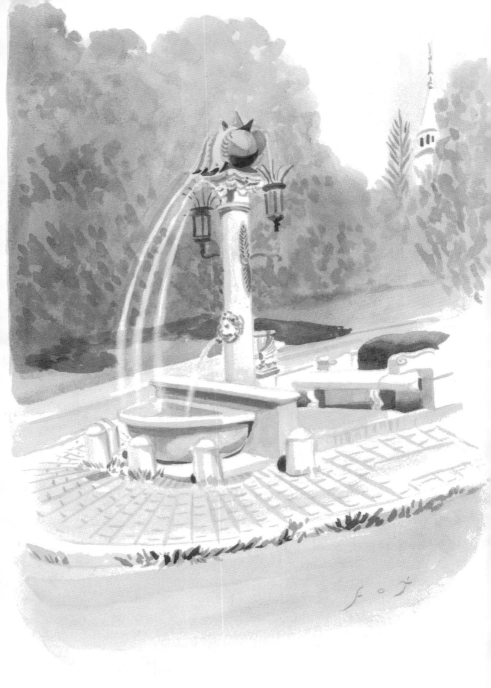

**FOUNTAIN FOR DOGS, HORSES & PEOPLE,
NORFOLK**

TOWER ON HAYSTACK MT., NORFOLK

stained glass windows. Go, by all means, and refresh yourselves by the sight of these glories of stained glass art.

Before we leave this storied town, we have two little adventures for you. Go north on Route 272 and soon on your left is a sign that says, "Litchfield Hills Haystack Mountain State Park." Head in, and when you can't drive anymore, park and follow a path through the woods. It's level for a while, then it starts up. There are stone steps for when the going gets rough, and blazes on the trees to guide you. It's a fairly long hike through the woods, but keep going. Soon you will break out and be at the base of a stone tower with a spiral stair at the top. When you get there and look out, there are 360 degrees of Berkshire beauty at your feet. For kids, the climb is a snap; for older people it's not, but you will be happy you made the effort.

Now back to your car and continue up Route 272. When you are nearly at the Massachusetts border you will be at the Campbell Falls State Park, a lovely place with walks through the woods, good places for picnics, and waterfalls for your cameras.

If you want to stay in this fabled town, we have places you should know about. On Maple Avenue on your left is a baronial house with mullioned windows. Called aptly Manor House, owned and operated by Hank and Diane Tremblay, an elegant bed and breakfast.

The interior is glowing and magnificent, and the rooms are graced with Tiffany stained glass windows. Everything about the house, including breakfast, is superb. The telephone is (203) 542-5690.

The Tremblays offer an unusual and useful service, a bed and breakfast reservation service that covers Connecticut, the Berkshires of Massachusetts, the Hudson River Valley of New York, the Rhode Island shoreline, and southern Vermont. They call this service the Covered Bridge. The number is (203) 542-5944.

Down Route 44 going west not very far is the big, beautiful 227-year-old Blackberry Inn, on the National Register of His-

FARM SCENE, NORFOLK

NOW, HIRAM, NOT SO FAST!

toric Places, a house where you will be treated in comfort and friendliness. It is a full service inn with fine rooms and excellent cuisine. The innkeeper is Kim Zukerman. There are 19 guest rooms, some with fireplaces. The telephone is (203) 542-5100.

The Mountain View, also a full service inn, is on a rise of ground on Route 272 as you go south, with lovely views over the valleys and hills of Norfolk. Michele Sloane is the owner of this lovely old house with its finely decorated interior and outstanding cuisine. The number is (203) 542-5595.

Another place you will be glad to know about is the Greenwoods on Greenwoods Road East (Route 44), the genius of Deanne Raymond, who has turned her Victorian house into an enchantment of beauty in comfort and elegance. The three suites are so richly and appealingly furnished and so home-like that many of Deanne's guests call the house their "home away from home." A prominent magazine has called it New England's most romantic bed and breakfast. The telephone is (203) 542-5439.

The ad says, "The best seats for viewing the fall color show are in the private carriages you can hire from Norfolk's Horse and Carriage Livery Service. Beth Denis and Judy Wiltse's equipages are spanking clean and their horses well groomed." Besides being available for whatever horse-drawn outing you have in mind, this service offers hayrides. It's a lovely way to beguile an afternoon or evening, so bring a picnic and a bottle. The telephone is (203) 542-6085.

So now, our explorer friends, we bow to you and bid you farewell with the hope that a kind providence will see you safely home and that you have enjoyed these tours in the Litchfield Hills as much as we, your guides.

DISCOVER THE COUNTRY WITH HIPPOCRENE U.S.A. GUIDES!

EXPLORING FLORIDA
ANNE RANKIN
Addressed to those who want to taste more of Florida than florid cocktails and Disneyworld, this enterprising guide explores lesser-known historic sites, natural attractions, and beaches.
0528 ISBN 0-87052-029-6 $16.95 paper

CHICAGOLAND AND BEYOND:
NATURE AND HISTORY WITH 200 MILES
GERALD and PATRICIA GUTEK
Over 80 family outings to suit all tastes and ages.
0718 ISBN 0-87052-036-9 $14.95 paper

By the same authors:
EXPLORING THE AMERICAN WEST:
A GUIDE TO MUSEUM VILLAGES
Featuring 30 sites in California, Arizona, New Mexico, Colorado, Wyoming, Oregon, and Washington. *"A wonderful source of historical information...a gold mine for travelers"*--Library Journal
0061 ISBN 0-87052-793-2 $11.95 paper

EXPLORING MID-AMERICA:
A GUIDE TO MUSEUM VILLAGES
Featuring 22 sites in Iowa, Minnesota, Kansas, Nebraska, the Dakotas, Arkansas, Oklahoma, and Texas.
0412 ISBN 0-87052-643-X $14.95 paper

AMERICA'S HEARTLAND:
A TRAVEL GUIDE TO THE BACKROADS OF ILLINOIS, INDIANA, IOWA, KANSAS AND MISSOURI (Expanded edition)
TOM WEIL
2320 ISBN 0-87052-038-5 $16.95 paper

By the same author:
AMERICA'S SOUTH:
A TRAVEL GUIDE TO THE ELEVEN SOUTHERN STATES
The only available single-volume guide covering Virginia, the Carolinas, Georgia, Alabama, Mississippi, Louisiana, Kentucky, Tennessee, Arkansas, and Florida. *"You'll enjoy this"*--St. Louis Home
0393 ISBN 0-87052-611-1 $17.95 paper

GUIDE TO BLACK AMERICA
MARCELLA THUM
Historic homes, art and history museums, parks, monuments, landmarks of the civil rights movement, battlefields and forts, colleges and churches throughout the United States.
0722 ISBN 0-87052-045-8 $11.95 paper

THE GUIDE TO BLACK WASHINGTON:
PLACES AND EVENTS OF HISTORICAL AND CULTURAL SIGNIFICANCE IN THE NATION'S CAPITAL
SANDRA FITZPATRICK and MARIA GOODWIN
"Wonderful"--Kathryn Smith, President, Washington Historical Society
0025 ISBN 0-87052-832-7 $14.95 paper

WEST POINT AND THE HUDSON VALLEY
GALE KOHLHAGEN and ELLEN HEINBACH
Foreword by GENERAL DAVE R. PALMER, SUPERINTENDENT OF WEST POINT
An insider's guide to the stories, sites, cadet life and lore of the U.S. Military Academy; with side trips to great estates, historic sites, and wineries.
0083 ISBN 0-87052-889-0 $14.95 paper

UNCOMMON AND UNHERALDED MUSEUMS
BEVERLY NARKIEWICZ and LINCOLN S. BATES
500 regional and thematic museums across the nation.
0052 ISBN 0-87052-956-0 $14.95 paper

THE SOUTHWEST:
A FAMILY ADVENTURE
TISH MINEAR and JANET LIMON
An imaginative guide exploring the Colorado Plateau through Utah, Colorado, Arizona, and New Mexico.
0394 ISBN 0-87052-640-5 $16.95 paper

RV:
TRAVEL LEISURELY YEAR ROUND
ROLANDA DUMAIS MASSE
Practical, first-hand advice on living in a recreational vehicle with independence and economy.
0058 ISBN 0-87052-958-7 $14.95 paper

LONG ISLAND:
A GUIDE TO NEW YORK'S SUFFOLK AND NASSAU COUNTIES (Revised)
RAYMOND, JUDITH and KATHRYN SPINZIA
0088 ISBN 0-87052-879-3 $17.50 paper